Your Child

Suzy Powling
Karen Christensen

Published 1990 by
Harrap Publishing Group Ltd
Chelsea House
26 Market Square
Bromley
Kent BR1 1NA
By arrangement with Amanuensis Books Ltd

ISBN 0 245-60011-6

This book was designed and produced by
Amanuensis Books Ltd
12 Station Road
Didcot
Oxfordshire OX11 7LL
UK

Editorial and art director: Loraine Fergusson
Senior editor: Lynne Gregory
Authenticator: Dr Hugh Pelly
Illustration: Loraine Fergusson, Ron Freeborn, Lynne Gregory, David Gifford
Cover design: Roger King Graphic Studios

MGI Prime Health, the health division of Municipal General Insurance Ltd, part of the Municipal Insurance Group, has contributed to the cost of this publication.

The information contained in this book has been obtained from professional medical sources and every care has been taken to ensure that it is consistent with current medical practice. However, it is intended only as a guide to current medical practice and not as a substitute for the advice of your medical practitioner which must, on all occasions, be taken.

Contents

Actual size
at 5 weeks

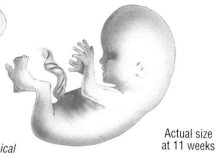

Actual size
at 7 weeks

Actual size
at 11 weeks

All the important physical characteristics of a human being are determined at the moment of conception. When the mother's egg is fertilized by the father's sperm, chromosomes from both parents are fused. The chromosomes carry the information - the genetic material - which fixes, for example, the sex, hair color and adult bodily physique of the child whose new life has just begun. The fertilized egg consists of a single cell, but it divides and multiplies very rapidly as it moves down the Fallopian tube towards the uterus (womb). At the end of the journey the mass of cells, looking rather like a blackberry, arrives ready to implant itself as an embryo in the wall of the uterus. At this point, the cells separate into distinct but united groups: those which burrow into the uterine wall eventually become the placenta, the vital link between mother and baby. The remainder divide into three layers; one is responsible for the formation of the brain, face, eyes, ears and skin; one for the skeleton, heart, kidneys and

sexual organs; and the third for the lungs and digestive organs. These highly significant events, which predetermine the condition of the child-to-be, take place within two to three weeks of fertilization.

Five to eight weeks
At five weeks the umbilical cord which connects the embryo to the placenta is being formed. Two or three weeks later it is possible to see where the baby's arms and legs, eyes and ears will be. Most important, the newly formed heart is beating strongly enough to be detected by the ultrasound scan.

Eight to ten weeks
From this stage the word 'fetus', meaning 'offspring', is used to describe the developing baby. The face is now more easily discernible, since the eyes have formed (though still covered by the eyelids), the jawline is clearer and tiny ears are visible. Fingers and toes can be recognized. The head makes

up about 50 per cent of the total size of the baby. Internal organs are almost completely formed.

Twelve to fourteen weeks
The enlarged uterus can be felt by a doctor at around this stage, even though most women will not look pregnant. By the end of the fourteenth week, however, the baby has completed its basic development and is moving freely in the amniotic fluid. This fills the uterine cavity, keeping the baby warm, protecting it from injury and providing fluid to drink.

Fourteen to twenty weeks
In this stage of pregnancy the fetus grows rapidly, and the relation of head to body size becomes more proportionate. The eyes are still closed; fine hair called lanugo appears on the body, and hair also begins to appear on the head.

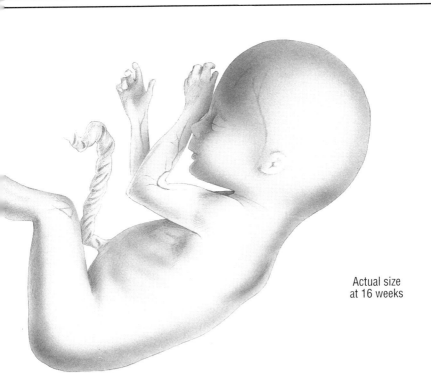

Actual size
at 16 weeks

Twenty to twenty-four weeks
The baby's fully formed organs continue to grow. Its skin is covered with a protective substance called vernix caseosa, fingernails appear and the nostrils open. The average weight at 24 weeks is 620 grams (1 lb 6 oz) and length 23 cm (9 inches) from the top of the head to the bottom of the back. This is the easiest measurement to take on ultrasound as the baby is usually in a curled-up position.

Twenty-four to thirty-two weeks
At 24 weeks hearing is well developed. Although the fetus is now heavier than the placenta, the latter still performs its essential tasks. These include supplying nutrients and oxygen to the fetus, removing waste products, producing hormones that maintain pregnancy and protecting the fetus from some, though not all, substances that might be dangerous. Harmful drugs that do cross the placenta include alcohol and nicotine. At 28 weeks the baby opens its eyes. If born prematurely at this stage it would be able

to breathe, but with great difficulty, as the lungs are immature. By 32 weeks the body has started to accumulate fat and the wrinkles present on the skin at 28 weeks are smoothing out.

Thirty-two to forty weeks
The brain, kidneys, lungs and digestive system are completely developed by 36 weeks. From this point the reflexes of sucking and swallowing are perfected and the baby's soft bones become firmer. After 40 weeks of pregnancy the baby is ready for life outside the protective sphere of the uterus.

Your child

The newborn baby

From the moment a baby is born, a new phase in development begins. While there are things he or she can do independently from the start, such as breathing, in many respects the baby is entirely dependent on the mother's assistance. If the baby is slow to breathe, perhaps as a side effect of analgesics (pain relief) given to the mother during labor, the pediatrician who is present at delivery may give some extra oxygen. Besides making sure that the baby has started to breathe properly, it is important to keep the baby warm. After birth the baby is wrapped in warm blankets then given to the mother to hold. Some places lay the baby naked on the mother's abdomen for a few minutes before wrapping.

The condition of a newborn baby is assessed for five features in particular which give a good index of well-being one and five minutes after birth: heart rate, respiratory rate, color activity and response to stimulation. A score of between zero and two, called the APGAR score (see left), is given for each feature. Babies with a low score may require simple resuscitation and respond very well. A few may be admitted to a special care unit for a matter of days. All babies are routinely weighed and measured at birth.

If a baby has any problems after delivery, they will naturally be dealt with straight away. The vast majority of babies are normal and healthy, and it is reassuring that a full physical check will be carried out by a pediatrician, a specialist in the care of infants, within a week of birth. This check ensures that nothing has been missed in earlier observations and that all the baby's systems are functioning as they should.

APGAR score:
Appearance (color)
Pulse (heart rate)
Grimace (irritability)
Activity (muscle power)
Respiration (breathing)

First physical examination

The baby's clothing and nappy will be removed for the examination, which should always takes place in the presence of the mother. The pediatrician will listen to the baby's heart and feel the pulse before proceeding to a detailed check-up.

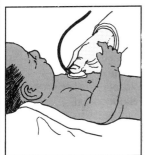
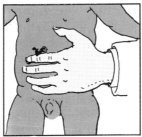
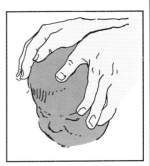

• Heart, lungs and pulses

Using a stethoscope, the pediatrician will listen to the heart back and front, observing the baby's breathing at the same time. Heart murmurs are often heard in newborn babies, but do not cause concern: a baby with a serious heart problem will look ill and will be identified by the pediatrician even before listening with the stethoscope. To check the pulses in the arteries to the legs, the pediatrician will feel the baby's groin.

• The genitals

Baby girls will be checked to see that the vagina and the urethral opening from the bladder are normally positioned. Boys will be examined to check that the penis is normal and that both testicles have descended. Even if they have not, no treatment is likely to be offered for at least 12 months, after which a simple operation can be performed.

• The abdomen

At the beginning of the examination, while the baby is still relaxed, the stomach will be felt gently to make sure there are no unusual swellings or lumps and that the organs are in the right place. If the umbilicus is inflamed or is not healing properly it will be noted and treatment prescribed if necessary.

• The spine and feet

Most babies' feet 'turn in', probably as a result of the position adopted in the womb, but they are flexible and can gently be moved to a normal position. The pediatrician will lift up the baby at this point to demonstrate the stepping reflex which the baby makes when held upright with the foot touching a surface. In this position the spine can be observed and the general muscle tone, which should be neither floppy nor too stiff, is evident.

• The head and mouth

The pediatrician will gently feel the baby's head for unusual swellings or abnormalities. There may be a swelling caused by a little bleeding around the bones of the skull during delivery. It takes a few weeks to subside but causes no problems. The baby's head will be measured now and at future medical check-ups as an indicator of growth rate.

A baby may have blisters on the lips caused by sucking, but these will clear up spontaneously. Thrush (see page 75) makes the mouth sore and is characterized by thick white patches on the tongue which can be eliminated with drops of an anti-fungal liquid administered after feeds. The pediatrician will use a small torch to examine inside the mouth and feel with a finger to make sure there is no cleft palate.

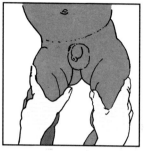

The hips

The pediatrician leaves until last the examination which may cause the baby some discomfort. The pediatrician is looking for congenital dislocation of the hips, which if undetected will lead to a serious limp, but which can be corrected if treated in the first few months of life with a splint or plaster cast.

To check the hips the pediatrician will place the baby on the back, hold the legs with the knees fully bent and turn the legs outwards. If the top of the thigh bone is not correctly placed in the hip socket this maneuver will not be possible. The baby's ligaments are sometimes a little soft (as a result of hormones transferred by the mother during pregnancy) and this can lead to 'clicking' around the hips in the first week or so, which fades away and is not serious.

Weight and length

The baby's measurements are taken at birth and provide the starting point for growth. All babies lose a little weight after birth and regain it within ten days. The correct weight for one baby may be rather different from another, taking into account genetic factors; small parents are likely to have small babies, for example. The average weight is 3.2 kg (just over 7 lb); boys are often 100-200 grams heavier and first babies lighter than second or later ones. Mothers who smoke have lighter babies; women with diabetes may have much heavier ones.

A baby's weight at birth, inherited factors considered, is an important indicator of his or her well-being, as it is throughout life. Regular checks on weight and height made in the early years show if your baby is developing as he or she should. Gaining weight and height - in other words, increasing in size - at a healthy rate is the key to growing well. Child health clinics record each baby's weight against charts which show the expected increase for so-called 'heavy', 'average', and 'light' babies, with different expectations for boys and girls. For example, a baby girl who was 'average' - 3.4 kg (7 lb 8 oz) and 53 cm (21 inches) - at birth should weigh 6.5 kg (14 lb 8 oz) and be just over 66 cm (26 inches) long at 20 weeks. There are inevitably going to be blips in the chart, but if your baby stays roughly on course you will know he or she is progressing well. If the weight curve takes off while length stays in line, you can see the danger of overweight before it gets out of hand, and similarly spot under-feeding if the rate of weight gain fails to keep pace with an increase in length.

Newborn characteristics

With a first baby especially, you will probably be acutely aware of anything in your baby's appearance that strikes you as less than perfect, such as a rash or a little bump on the head, and be sensitive to every sound or move made. Expectations of a perfect, smooth, contented baby are unlikely to be met in the first few days of life: consider what an enormous adjustment has been made from the protective environment of the peaceful womb, to a world full of strange sounds, sights and people, as well as coping with eating and breathing.

The skin

Rashes on newborn babies are extremely common. The skin is one of our most sensitive organs and, throughout life, reacts quickly to changes in environment and diet. Toxic erythema or neonatal urticaria is the name given to a rash of tiny white spots on a red surrounding area that appears on the baby's body, occasionally on the arms and legs. It is not a sign of infection and clears up without treatment within a few days. Little cream spots on the face, called milia, are equally innocuous but may persist for two to three weeks before clearing up. Some full-term babies or those who are a little late arriving may have dry, flaky skin rather than the peachy bloom you had expected. Rubbing in a light baby oil will soon make the skin softer.

You may be worried about the tone of your baby's skin color: sometimes the normal pink is stained yellow or brown if the baby experienced some distress before or during delivery and opened the bowels (passed meconium) in the womb. This fades within days. Babies of Afro-Caribbean parents are quite pale at birth but their skin pigmentation quickly increases.

Don't be concerned if your baby looks paler when asleep: this is normal and natural.

Often a baby who has been of a normal pink color turns yellowish during the first week. This is caused by jaundice and is very common. Because the baby's liver is immature it is not very efficient at dealing with a substance called bilirubin which is a by-product of the breakdown of hemoglobin in the red blood cells. In adults bilirubin is normally excreted. Jaundice of this kind usually clears up during the second week, or third week with premature babies. Jaundice is easily treated with phototherapy (light treatment). The baby is placed naked in a cot under a special ultra-violet light, with a pad over the eyes to protect them. The light breaks down the yellow pigment in the skin so that the baby can excrete it

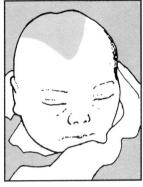

Cradle cap (seborrheic dermatitis of the scalp) manifests itself as scaly crusts on the head. This condition clears up within a few months if left alone. If you find it unsightly, however, rub a little baby oil into the crusts to soften them overnight, then gently remove them with a comb. Shampoo regularly with a mild medicated shampoo.

'Stork marks' are small pink marks that appear after a day or two on the back of the neck and the eyelids and usually fade away in a few weeks. Birthmarks that are present at birth, such as flat red patches on the side of the face, are caused by an abnormality of the capillary blood vessels in the area and may persist. If you discuss this with your pediatrician he or she will reassure you that such marks cause no skin problems and will advise you on dealing with them.

in the normal way. If a blood test reveals excessively high levels of bilirubin the pediatrician will investigate whether the baby has an infection or there is an incompatibility between your blood group and the baby's.

Most Afro-Caribbean and Asian babies have a grey mark at the base of the spine known as 'Mongolian blue spot', which again is harmless and disappears in the first two years.

The head

Babies born by Caesarian section or those who were delivered in the breech position will probably have a nicely rounded head. In a normal, vaginal delivery, however, the baby's head is somewhat elongated because it has moulded itself to the shape of the birth canal. It settles back to normal very quickly. Because the head has to be moulded in this way the bones of the baby's skull are mobile: at the top and back of the head where the bones have not yet joined, the head is covered with a protective membrane. The gaps between the bones are called fontanelles, and the one at the front - the anterior fontanelle or 'soft spot' - takes quite a while to close up, possibly as long as 18 months. You can sometimes see the soft spot pulsating, but although it seems very tender you can be sure it is perfectly strong and it is quite safe to touch it.

The instruments used in a forceps delivery may leave slight marks on your baby's head, but these disappear quickly and are not signs of injury: forceps are used to protect your baby from harm, not to cause it. Similarly the suction cap of a vacuum (Ventouse) may leave slight swelling on the crown of the head which causes no problems and quickly subsides.

Baby's breasts

Boys and girls alike may have slightly swollen breasts, and even discharge a little milk during the first few weeks of life. While in the womb, the baby is absorbing female hormones which have this effect, which is temporary and requires no treatment. Don't be tempted to try to squeeze the milk out as this could cause an infection.

Hair

The amount of hair on a baby's head is no indicator of crowning glory to come. Those who are almost bald will eventually have a full head of hair, while babies with thick hair often lose it all before it grows again. Lanugo (downy hair on the body) is usually only obvious on premature babies and disappears as the baby gains weight.

Hiccups and sneezes

Some new babies hiccup frequently (as they do in the womb) but this does not distress them or prevent them from sucking and enjoying a feed. Hiccups disappear as the baby settles down to a daily rhythm of sleeping and feeding. Bouts of sneezing are not a problem either, and - unless other symptoms are obvious - are not a sign of a cold or infection. Since a baby can't blow the nose, sneezing is nature's way of doing it.

Eyes

Babies tend to have deep blue eyes, the true eye color developing over the first year. During the first few weeks, a squint may be apparent, because the muscles which coordinate eye movements are not fully developed. This usually rights itself within three months or so. Part of every developmental check includes a sight test, and a persistent squint that needs treatment will be picked up by the doctor.

'Sticky eyes' is the term usually used to describe a yellowish discharge from the eyes of a newborn baby. A test will be carried out to make sure it is not caused by a bacterial infection. Usually it is not, and simply cleansing the eyes regularly with clean cotton wool and a saline (salt) solution will clear it up. Always use a separate cotton wool swab for each eye and wipe from the inside outwards. A recurrent discharge, making the eyes red and sore, may be caused by conjunctivitis, and the doctor will want to treat this with an antibiotic ointment.

Bowel movements

A baby usually opens the bowels in the first day of life, producing meconium. This odorless, dark green substance which was contained in the fetus's bowel is gradually replaced by brownish-yellow stools as the residue of milk feeds. The stools of a breastfed baby are soft, almost odorless and usually yellow. In a baby whose digestive system is just getting going, stools that are greenish in colour are not unusual and should not alarm you unless the baby is otherwise fretful, feverish or lacking in appetite. If your baby is being bottle-fed, the stools will be browner, more smelly and less frequent. Curds in the

The action of sucking stimulates the milk sacs (alveoli) in the breast to squeeze milk down through the milk ducts and into the nipple. This is felt as a tingling sensation and is known as the 'let-down' or 'draught' reflex. Some mothers find that when breastfeeding is established simply hearing their baby cry or even thinking about him or her when temporarily separated is enough to set the reflex off (which is why it is wise to line your bra with breast pads when you're going out!).

stool are simply undigested protein from the cow's milk on which bottle feeds are based, and are not a cause for concern.

Feeding
Babies in the womb suck their thumbs. This primitive sucking reflex, which is present at birth, is one of the most important for survival. Most women are pleased to see their baby latch on to the breast within minutes of birth. Related to this is the 'rooting' reflex which stimulates new babies to search for the nipple: a light touch at the side of the mouth and your baby will turn the head and open the mouth to receive food. This action stimulates a corresponding reflex in the mother so that she will produce milk to satisfy her baby's hunger. No special preparation is needed for breastfeeding. The action of the hormone prolactin means that the breasts start to produce milk naturally after your baby is born. The more often the baby is put to the breast, the more hormone is produced and the greater becomes the milk supply.

Whether you breast or bottle feed your baby, feeding 'on demand' in the early days is the best method. Let the baby, not the clock, decide how often to feed for and how long. Sucking is important and pleasurable to babies, and soon a routine of more or less four-hourly feeds will establish itself without imposing any rigid management policy. Night feeds are inevitably part of this pattern while the baby's digestive system can only cope with relatively small amounts at a time.

Sleeping patterns
A newborn baby has no concept of day and night: this is an idea which is gradually picked up from the routines of daily life. Nevertheless he or she will on most days demonstrate a pattern of sleeping and wakeful periods centred on feeding times. There is very little you can do to change the proportion of the day your baby needs to sleep - and there are differences. Some new babies sleep as many as 18 hours to start with, waking only to feed. Others are much more wakeful: this is a matter of

temperament, not bad management. You can reinforce the idea of 'night' and 'day' as the weeks pass with routines such as an evening bath or morning playtime. At night-time, make the circumstances for sleep as congenial as possible: the room should be warm, with dim lights (so that you can see to feed and change the baby in the night), and reasonably quiet - though the whole house need not be plunged into silence just because the baby's gone to bed. Wrap the baby securely in a soft blanket and place one or two light blankets on top. Do not use a pillow: it is unnecessary and might cover your baby's face. Different babies sleep in different positions, but many seem to be comfortable on their stomachs. Do not put your baby down on the back after a feed because the baby may have trouble coping with regurgitated milk in this position.

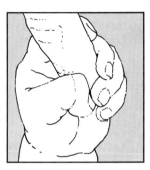

Everyone is fascinated by the miniature perfection of a tiny baby's beautiful hands, and delighted by the determination with which the baby holds on to an adult finger. This grip is not consciously made, however, but is a result of the 'grasp' reflex, which a baby is born with. A newborn baby's hands are held closed much of the time but within three months - by which point the grasp reflex has disappeared - they have opened up.

Milestones in physical development

A newborn baby is capable of few directed movements. If placed in the cot, the baby will remain in the same position, moving the arms and legs a little, waving the hands and wiggling the toes weakly. It is only a matter of months before this placid creature is well on the way to becoming an active toddler, interested in everything that's going on. This development is composed of a number of different but intimately related factors.

Head control

When you lift up a new baby you must always support the head carefully, as the neck and back muscles are not strong enough to take its weight. Control of the head comes as these muscles strengthen, simultaneously increasing your baby's power to move the legs and arms. If your baby is lying on the tummy, the legs are drawn up and he or she cannot lift the head up from the mattress. By six weeks many babies can do this, and will be able to stretch their legs out and move their arms more vigorously. At three months the muscles are so strong that your baby can raise the head and shoulders and have a good look around. After another month the baby can push up with

Pediatrician
A specialist in the care of babies and children and the diseases of childhood. A pediatrician will not always be present at a normal delivery, but will certainly be in the delivery room in the event of twins, a breech or other abnormal presentation or if delivery is by Caesarian section. If there is any sign of fetal distress during labor the pediatrician will be on hand to care for the baby as soon as he or she is born. Before leaving hospital, all babies are given a thorough check-up (see pages 6-10) by a pediatrician. Pediatricians work mainly in hospitals but also in child health clinics and community health centres.

Midwife
A Registered General Nurse (RGN) who has undertaken further training to become a State Certified Midwife (SCM). During your ante-natal visits to the hospital you will be seen by a midwife as well as an obstetrician (a doctor who specializes in the care of pregnant women and their unborn babies). If you are receiving ante-natal care from your general practitioner you will probably be examined by the midwife attached to the practice at each visit, building up a relationship which can be very supportive during labor and when you are learning to

the hands. By this stage head control is such that, if you raise your baby to a sitting position from lying prone, he or she can stop the head falling back. The ability to hold the head in line with the spine is a prelude to mastery of the balance required to sit unaided.

As control over the head increases, your baby abandons the curled-up 'fetal' position of the newborn and straightens out. When on the back, he or she practises moving the arms and legs - with particular vigor when the restrictions of a nappy are removed. These kicking movements, rather like bicycling in the air, are both a sign of increasing strength and a means of increasing it further still. The ability to sit unaided needs strong leg, back and neck muscles.

You will see your baby trying very hard to sit up before he or she can actually make it. A favorite game is being taken by the hands and raised to a sitting position. At this stage you can leave your baby propped up (but not unattended) for increasingly longer periods of time, supported by a pillow under the mattress of the pram or cot, or in a baby-chair with a restraint between the legs and round the waist. Adjustable chairs are excellent as they can be moved from an almost reclining position to the near-vertical by stages according to your baby's needs. By the end of the six-month period your baby can be propped almost upright, and may even be able to sit unaided for a second or two.

Development of sight

At birth your baby can see clearly to a range of about 25 cm (10 inches) - the distance separating your faces when you're feeding. Further than that a baby is aware of light and shade and movement. The baby's own hands too are endlessly fascinating. As head control improves he or she can turn to look at a moving object, and by six months, with greater focussing power, the baby will look around with alertness for a toy worthy of attention.

Hand and eye coordination

If you put a small toy in a newborn's hand, he or she will

grab it firmly. The baby will swipe out at a string of toys suspended across the pram or crib, but the movements are not at all precise. By six months a baby can transfer an object from one hand to another, but is more likely to put it to the mouth, which is why he or she should never be allowed small toys.The increasing ability to hold an object of choice deliberately and to focus clearly on individual items work together to refine the combined skills of seeing, selecting and picking up that object. This physical skill is crucial to intellectual development and indeed vitally important throughout life. (Adult skills such as driving a car are dependent on good coordination.) Stimulate this skill by providing simple toys that will engage your baby's attention.

Hearing and speech

At the earliest stages of development the connection between hearing and learning to speak is less obvious than it is in a toddler, but a normal newborn baby can hear perfectly well. What takes a little time is for him or her to understand what certain sounds mean. Sudden loud noises will startle a baby, sometimes provoking what has been called the Moro response(when a baby throws out both arms and legs). This reflex disappears after about three months. By contrast the sound of his mother's or father's voice will be comforting and familiar. By the end of the six-month period he or she will recognize other welcome sounds like dinner being prepared and react with pleasure.

From very early days your baby will try to communicate with you: letting you know when he or she is hungry or tired or lonely with an appropriate cry. The sounds a baby makes at about two months are a prelude to true speech: vowel sounds like 'aa' and 'ee'. Your baby may not understand your words in this early period, but speaking to him or her is an important part of communication. The sound of your voice delights and interests your baby and listening to it is one of the key factors in learning to speak.

care for your baby. The normal delivery of a baby in hospital is undertaken by a midwife who will call in an obstetrician if complications arise, such as the need to use forceps.

The midwives are responsible for both mother and baby for the duration of their time in hospital, and after that, when you get home, for a period of ten days.

Health visitor
An RGN with midwifery experience who is further trained in all aspects of community care, both social and medical. When the midwife's period of care ends at ten days after delivery, the health visitor assumes responsibility for you and your baby. Health visitors run your local child health clinic which is often attached to a group of general practitioners, with whom they conduct development assessment clinics. A health visitor will make the first call on you at home and will call again occasionally in the early weeks or at any time you would like a visit. Health visitors are tremendously experienced in all aspects of family health and will be a great source of support and information to you.

Physical development

The Community Health Center

In each area there are centers in which various aspects of health care are grouped together, one of which is the child health clinic. You are advised to visit your clinic at regular intervals when your baby is very small for weighing and to give you an opportunity to discuss with the health visitors any aspect of your baby's well-being that concerns you. You can obtain vitamin drops at the clinic if need be. Immunizations are given at the clinic when required: the clinic will notify you when they are due and ask you to bring your child at an appropriate time. The health visitor and pediatrician will usually carry out development assessment checks at the clinic. Some health centers have mother-and-baby groups that meet regularly, where you can get together with other women in the same situation as yourself on a social basis. Even if your center does not have one, your health visitor is sure to know of such groups that exist in your district and can also advise on matters such as day nurseries or child-minders if you need to return to work.

Six months to one year

Muscular control starts at the head and moves down, so that by about six months your baby can hold the head up and use the shoulders, arms and hands well. He or she may be able to sit unsupported for a few seconds, no longer. By eight months some babies lean forward and rest on their hands for support, but this isn't much fun as they cannot use their hands for playing. At this stage you can help your baby practise sitting, either by pulling him or her up by the hands, or getting the baby into position snugly surrounded by pillows or rolled-up blankets. Do not leave your baby alone, even with the cushions, as he or she could fall face forward and smother.

The muscular strength in the legs that leads to sitting unaided also permits your baby to crawl. This stage is usually reached at about ten months, sometimes later, and some babies dispense with crawling altogether, preferring to maneuver themselves around by shuffling on their bottoms, though using hands and arms is still a more efficient means of getting around. Arriving at the crawling position happens after experiments with rocking from side to side, rolling over and wriggling on the stomach.

Part of the motivation to crawl is a desire to follow you around; part of it a desire to hold something that is out of reach - a cuddly toy or a rattle. At six months a baby can focus on an object at almost any distance and reach out for it. Crawling brings a whole new world of interesting items into his or her sphere, and it is important to make sure harmful objects are cleared aside.

Hand control in this second half-year develops at a tremendous pace, leading from relatively clumsy, but successful, attempts at picking things up with the whole hand, to the refinement of using the index finger and thumb to hold an object as small as a pea. Having learned to pick things up, at about nine months your baby masters the corresponding art of letting them go, which involves consciously relaxing the hand muscles. This, to a baby, has wondrous results, heralding a period of dropping anything that comes to hand on the floor.

Weight gain

Until your baby is six months old, your health visitor will probably recommend weekly weighing if possible. If all is going well, by the sixth month these regular checks can be less frequent, say once a month. The rate of weight gain, which is about 200 grams (7 oz) weekly in the first three months and about 112-142 grams (4-5 oz) weekly between three and six months, continues to slow down, and can now be expected to be about 56-85 grams (2-3 oz) every week. The corresponding increase in height will be about 10 cm (4 inches) by the end of the first year. As always, there will be little peaks and troughs on the chart caused either by minor illnesses that reduce your baby's appetite or enthusiasms for favorite foods when you introduce solid foods, encouraging him or her to eat more. As long as there is a regular increase at the expected rate you have nothing to worry about.

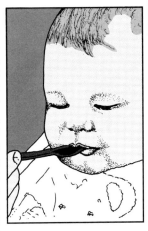

Solid foods given on a spoon are a necessary new experience for a baby who is accustomed - and attached - to the breast or bottle. It is not surprising that first attempts often meet with little success: so start by offering a very small spoonful of the new food while your baby is still adequately nourished by milk alone, just to get him or her used to the idea and to find out by trying a variety of foods which ones appeal the most.

Introducing solid foods

'Solid' is not a very accurate term to describe the first non-milk food introduced into a baby's diet, since an almost liquid consistency is preferable and can most easily be coped with. There is no fixed rule about what age to offer solids, except that you should not do so before your baby is three months old: the digestive system is not ready for them. By the time your baby achieves 5.5 kg (12 lb) in weight, a discrepancy appears between the amount of calories needed and the amount that can be got from daily milk. As the intervals between feeds grow longer and the number of daily feeds diminishes from six to five or even four, the amount of nourishment given at those feeds must increase to keep pace with your growing baby's demands. Even tiny amounts of solid foods can provide a great many extra calories. Do not reduce the amount of milk at this stage.

Once your baby has accepted a proportion of solid food the enthusiasm soon extends to joining in at mealtimes, so let the baby have a spoon. While you concentrate on getting some food into his or her mouth the baby can also experiment. The more practice he or

Bowel movements

A change in diet inevitably has an effect on the number and type of your baby's bowel movements. Solid foods, and cow's milk, are more demanding on the digestive system than breast milk or bottle feeds, and a greater proportion leaves the body as waste. In normal circumstances this will simply mean your baby soils the nappy less often and the stool is more like that of an adult. Constipation manifests itself as a dry, hard motion which is difficult to pass, and can be treated simply by giving your baby extra drinks, particularly fruit juice. Laxatives are unnecessary and should never be used unless prescribed by a doctor. Diarrhea is unlikely to be caused by the introduction of solid foods, though excessive sugar will produce a looser stool.

she gets, the sooner the baby will be enjoying an important measure of independence. This process is enhanced by offering finger-foods, such as carrot or rusk, which will be treated as a suckable toy at first, until it is realized that they are tasty as well.

Although your baby has no or few teeth at this stage, it is very good for the gums and jaw to be exercised by gnawing on foods such as these. Do not leave your baby unattended when eating.

Sleeping patterns

Up until about nine months old, your baby's pattern of sleeping and waking is governed entirely by need: when tired, he or she will fall asleep, and when the baby has had enough sleep, he or she will wake up. Generally this means a long sleep at night, once the night feed has been dropped, lasting on average about 12 hours. During the day the baby may have a couple of naps, which may last 30 minutes, two hours or more. Your baby's particular sleep requirements will not change, in so far as a baby who has always needed a good deal of sleep will continue to do so, and one who is wakeful most of the day will do the same.

At nine months or so your baby begins to have the ability to resist sleep, particularly at night and probably because he or she doesn't want to be separated from you. Very many parents have problems at about this stage, and a number of strategies have evolved for dealing with themt: after all, by mid-evening (if not earlier) your baby probably needs to be asleep and you most certainly need some time on your own.

If you have established bedtime routines in babyhood, such as a bath and play before bed, it will help to keep these up, maybe adapting them a little. Perhaps give the bath earlier, so that there is time for your baby to have a last snack in your company before being tucked in with a favorite toy. Stay with him or her for a set period, say 15 minutes, reading a story. Routines and rituals spell security to a child. With this in mind, the hour preceding bedtime should be free from stress. It's a perfect time for parents who have been out at work all day to spend with their baby playing quietly and chatting. When the time for sleep comes, make sure the baby is warm enough and not likely to be disturbed by outside noises, as the baby will sleep more lightly now than during the first few months. If he or she gains comfort from cuddling an old blanket or item of your clothing, or from thumbsucking, that's fine.

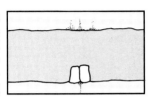

Approximately six months

Often babies who go to sleep happily enough, wake up several times in the night. If the last meal of the day has been satisfying enough, this is unlikely to be caused by hunger, although a little drink may be welcome, and often a cuddle is all that is needed. If that doesn't do the trick, it may be that your baby is uncomfortable in a wet nappy (especially if there is nappy rash) and will settle down once clean and dry. Keep these night wakings as brief and business-like as possible: don't let your baby sense an opportunity for midnight games!

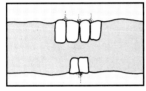

Approximately eight months

Daytime naps are still a part of the sleeping pattern, whether it's two long ones or two half-hour catnaps. Even if your baby can go without one of the long naps, it is still a good idea to have a 'rest' period set aside, when the baby stays in the cot or pram for half an hour, warm, quiet and comfortable with one or two favourite toys.

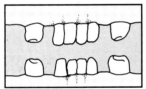

Approximately ten to fourteen months

Some babies won't want to be left like this if they're not actually tired enough to sleep. In these circumstances it is best not to persist, as the cot or pram will begin to be seen as a place of punishment rather than a haven of rest. It may help if you are in the room at the same time (you're almost certain to need a bit of a rest yourself), perhaps reading the paper or having a cup of tea. Companionable times like these can become a very rewarding part of your family life.

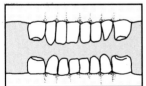

Approximately eighteen to thirty months

Teething

The age at which babies cut their first teeth varies enormously: some have no teeth at their first birthday, and at the other extreme, some are born with a tooth. The order in which teeth appear, however, almost always follows the pattern described overleaf. As a very

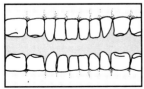

Approximately six years

Usual order of appearance of teeth:

1 Lower front teeth
2 Upper front teeth
3 Upper side teeth
4 Lower side teeth
5 First upper molars
6 First lower molars
7 Upper eye teeth
8 Lower eye teeth
9 Second lower molars
10 Second upper molars

approximate average, teething begins at about six months, and all 20 first teeth are usually through by two years old.

Teething can certainly cause soreness, but the only symptoms other than misery at the pain is dribbling. Any symptoms such as diarrhea, loss of appetite or raised temperature will have another cause and should be referred to your doctor. A carrot or rusk to gnaw on often helps. A teething ring cooled in the refrigerator is soothing, but beware of placing water-filled teething rings in the freezer. They can become so cold that they 'ice-burn' your baby's gums. Thankfully, some babies have very little trouble cutting their teeth. If your baby is unfortunate enough to suffer in the process, resist over-using painkillers or you will be giving an excess of medication in a short period of life when simple remedies are just as helpful. Try rubbing the gums with your little finger, and just be generally attentive and comforting.

Eventually your child will have to take care of his or her own teeth. You can establish good teeth-cleaning habits very early by giving your child a small soft toothbrush and letting him or her play at toothbrushing in imitation of you. Give the teeth a proper clean yourself once or twice a day, using a fluoride toothpaste (not the sweetened kind on sale for children). It is now known that it is just as important to take care of the 'milk' or first teeth as of the permanent teeth. As well as cleaning the teeth, the most important factor in preventing decay is a diet as free of sugar and sugary foods as possible: no sweet drinks, chocolate, sweets, biscuits or cakes is the ideal. Some children's medicines include sugar to make them more palatable, so always clean your child's teeth after administering syrups of this kind. Make sure the diet includes foods rich in calcium and vitamin D, such as dairy produce and oily fish like sardines.

You can start taking your baby to the dentist for check-ups at about two years old. Before that, take him or her with you when you have your own check-ups if possible and if your dentist has no objections. Your child can get used to the surgery and see from your example that there's nothing to be afraid of.

One year to two-and-a-half

Learning to walk is a difficult skill to master, calling for not only physical strength but sophisticated muscular coordination.

Before making the first steps, your baby has to be able to stand. This is an indication that the muscular control that started at the top, with the ability to hold up the head, has finally reached the feet. During the second half of the first year, he or she will have progressed from making 'knee-bend' movements when standing on your lap to little dance steps, lifting one foot and placing it on top of the other. If you hold the hands firmly your baby will soon be able to take a few steps on the floor with your support. It is not long before the child can stand alone taking weight but still needing your help with balance. Practising on anything that comes to hand - the bars of the cot, a heavy piece of furniture, your trouser-leg - he or she will hoist up to standing position, only to find that sitting down again is impossible. You are needed again for that, and the shouting will let you know.

From standing up, leaning on the sofa or coffee-table, it's a matter of weeks before your baby realizes he or she can shuffle along with feet and hands and move. This stage is known as 'cruising'.

Cruising

The more opportunities your baby has for experimenting safely in this period the better. Your baby will stumble often, but always try again, it's important for him or her to feel safe in one field of endeavour before launching into another. Cruising eventually leads to the ability to cross small gaps between supports, so that he or she can move from the sofa to the chair, to a low table, to your arms, and circumnavigate the room. At the next stage larger gaps between supports are coped with by taking two or three tottering steps, finally setting off in a determined way whether or not there is support to rely on.

Always remember that learning to walk requires great confidence. To achieve that your baby must have the experience of a safe environment in which to practise the first steps. Be careful of slippery floors, furniture that might give way if held onto, and older, boisterous children who can easily knock the baby off balance.

Like other developmental 'milestones', walking

While a baby of this age can manage to walk upstairs, he or she should not be left to manage alone. The ability to walk downstairs comes at about two years - meanwhile you can teach the safe way to get down: backwards.

comes at different times to different children. Most will be 'cruising' at the end of the first year, but a significant number will not do so until past their first birthday. By fifteen months the vast majority have taken their first independent steps, even if the ability to get up from the sitting position to standing upright does not come until 18 months. By this stage they will be walking more steadily, no longer needing to spread their arms out for balance.

Control over walking is still limited: your eighteen-month-old can move forward well enough, but cannot change direction suddenly to avoid a collision or walk backwards. By the second birthday a child is able to walk backwards, perhaps run and jump, and turn his or her head while running without losing balance. Running and jumping games in the garden or football in the park are great activities for two-year-olds that increase physical coordination and confidence.

Potty training

The phrase 'toilet training' implies that your baby can be taught to use the lavatory: but a child cannot learn to do this until the body is ready. That means waiting until he or she can control the muscles of the bowel and rectum, recognizing the signals that urination is necessary. Similarly with the bladder, which in babyhood is not mature enough to hold more than half a cupful of urine without emptying spontaneously. This degree of physical development is not going to happen until at least fifteen months of age, possibly much later, and there is no point in trying to get your child to use the potty before then. Trying to *make* your child use the potty at any stage is a great mistake. There's no harm in having a potty around a few months in advance, so that a child can get used to it and even get an idea of its purpose; but don't force him or her to sit on it. If an experimental potty session happens to coincide with a bowel movement, you've got one less nappy to wash, but don't take this as a signal to start earnest pottying. It is important to have a relaxed attitude about the achievement of bladder and bowel control; after all, no amount of worry and effort can accelerate a natural process governed by natural laws. An obsessive attitude, on the other hand, can communicate itself to your child and seriously hinder that process.

You will know when the moment has come to start introducing the potty with serious intent when it is clear that your child is aware that he or she has just emptied the bowels or is about to do so. You may be able to predict this to some extent if this usually happens at about the same time every day, and use your foreknowledge to suggest using the potty this time. Dress your child in clothes that are easy to get out of, so that the procedure is not too complicated. And if you are met with a refusal, don't push it. Leave it for a few days and be casual about it the next time.

When your child is successful, show you are pleased, bearing in mind that if you overdo your delight there may be some surprise that you so quickly deposit this object of triumph down the lavatory. Similarly, don't show any signs of disappointment if he or she does not perform on time: your child is more interested in pleasing you than using the potty and will be upset suspecting failure in your eyes. As in all things, a child needs your love and encouragement.

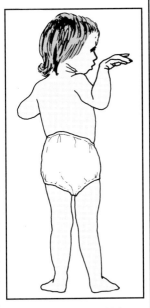

Trainer pants have a thick terry toweling inside and a waterproof outer layer.

Control of the bladder takes rather longer than bowel control. When you discover that your child has a completely dry nappy after the afternoon nap, for example, you can ask him or her to use the potty to empty the bladder before putting your child down for a nap the next day. This will become a routine that makes the purpose of the potty familiar, and you can gradually extend it throughout the day so that nappies become unnecessary. You can use special 'trainer pants' for an interim period. Unlike nappies, they will enable your child to feel when it is wet or dirty - and your carpet will be protected from accidents! Accidents are inevitable at this stage, when your child is likely to be so absorbed in a game he or she will completely forget about emptying the bladder. It's up to you to be forgiving when this happens, and to forestall it by suggesting the potty from time to time and when you can see from fidgeting and wriggling that your

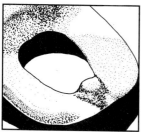

Using the adult lavatory
The transition from using the pot to the lavatory will probably happen fairly naturally, if gradually, as your child tries to do what he or she sees you doing. Make it easier by providing a little box to get up to the right level. Child's seats that fit over the lavatory seat (above) are not necessary but some children feel more secure with one of these. Show your child how to clean with toilet paper. Girls should always wipe from the front of the vulva backwards to prevent germs entering the vagina. Enforce the rule of washing hands after every visit to the lavatory.

child really needs to go. If you go out for any length of time take the potty with you so that your child can go without delay.

By the age of two, the majority of toddlers will be dry during the day, with a little bit of encouragement from you. Help by putting the child on the pot before naps, bedtime and first thing in the morning. Becoming dry at night takes rather longer. After all, during the day your child can go to the lavatory whenever he or she feels like it: during a long, heavy sleep the child will not notice an urgently full bladder and will wet the bed. As well as potting before bed, do it again before you go to bed yourself. Girls tend to be dry at night sooner than boys, but they almost all get there in the end, usually in the third year but sometimes a year later. A doctor would not consider treatment until a child was over five.

Learning

A baby is learning from the moment of birth: learning to recognize sights and sounds and work out what they mean, for example, as well as learning to use a developing body. Children are endlessly curious, adventurous and persistent, brimming with the qualities that enhance the learning process at any stage in life. Encourage them now and you are laying the foundations for many rich experiences later.

Each stage of physical development makes possible a further intellectual step: curiosity about an object can be satisfied once the child is able to walk to it, pick it up, examine it and possibly take it apart. It's fun but it is also learning. For the baby and young child, to live is to learn. While the immediate environment of your home is of great interest to your child, by no means everything in it can safely be subjected to scrutiny, whether because objects are too precious or because they are too dangerous. Even so, much satisfaction can be derived from playing with simple things: helping you unpack the shopping and sorting out the oranges, the apples and the potatoes; trying to pile them up like bricks and discovering it can't be done. Games like these are part of the process of differentiating between things, a crucial first step in the sorting process at the foundation of logical thought.

Speech

Hand-in-hand with efforts to separate out the bewildering variety of things that fill the world go attempts at speech. Your child is desperate to communicate with you, and you can help by communicating all the time, with gestures and touch as well as language. Acquiring a vocabulary will have started by the age of one, with the purpose of naming all the familiar and wished-for things in your child's sphere of experience: parents, bottle, biscuit, comfort blanket. As well as the parts of the child's own body, ritually ticked off at bathtime, each new experience must have its name: puddle, sand, shoes, bus.

As confidence in the meaning of words increases, the child will use them with intonations that underline their significance in a particular situation. When the family cat steals a fish finger from the table, for example, 'Ginger!' will ring out in disapproval. These first efforts at language must be supported by you, letting your child know that you have understood and agreed with what has been said. While in this experimental stage the child will use a word he or she already knows and pin it on a new object, calling a cow a horse, for example. Say the new name and you have not only increased his or her vocabulary, but more importantly, an understanding of the world and what happens in it.

Baby talk

'Baby talk' is bound to be used for a handful of favorite, intimate things or people. It is counter-productive if your child has to unlearn words like 'geegee' or 'bikbik' when school approaches and you don't want him or her to sound silly. If you use 'horse' and 'biscuit' from the start when speaking, your child will eventually drop the baby word in preference for yours without any need for conscious correction.

Sentence construction evolves gradually. You can detect that your child has grasped the basics by noting the

First attempts at making sentences consist of two words such as 'Daddy car', which could mean Daddy has just got home, just got in the car or is washing it, depending on circumstances. In your response, expand on what your child has said to reinforce the meaning and increase the sense of communication: 'Yes, the car will be lovely and clean when Daddy's finished'.

order in which he states his choice of words. Children listen closely to you, then model their sentences on yours, so that 'tired Pussy' will mean that the cat is asleep but 'Pussy dinner' that she's eating. Children build on this basic structure with increasingly complex strings of words to get the meaning over. Communicating is the point of the exercise, and it's too soon to start correcting grammatical errors like 'she been out' or 'I eated my apple'. Being corrected at this stage is discouraging. You may have to interpret when your child speaks to others, and vice versa, making smoother the experience of dealing with people outside the immediate family.

Becoming a social animal

While the beginnings of sociability show themselves in this period in a way adults can recognize easily, the capacity for enjoying the company of others begins in the first weeks of life. A baby who starts out with a secure and loving relationship with a mother, then with the other members of the family, seeks to perpetuate the pleasure engendered by these early relationships by forming bonds with others as time goes by.

Your baby's social achievements can be charted in the first year from an obvious desire to be picked up, smiles of recognition as you draw near, and, by about six months, expressions of apprehension at the sight of a strange face. The way babies behave is governed as much by individual personality as by common patterns, and you, the parents, will know your baby's character better than anyone.

Inevitably a quiet baby will be more content alone for short periods of time than a lively one: these traits must be respected. Knowing this, you can decide if your toddler will be sturdy enough to cope with a playgroup morning or happier going with you when you visit a friend for coffee. The best way to encourage a timid child to come out of his or her shell is to do so gradually, always in a familiar environment, until confidence grows.

Learning to interact with others is vital to development. Your baby learns to cope with a social circle that increases little by little until by the end of the first year your child feels happy not only with the immediate family but uncles and aunts and cousins as well as regular visitors to the house.

There are a number of ways in which you can introduce your toddler to other children of the same age: with luck you will have neighbors with children, or other children in your extended family, and there is sure to be a mother-and-toddler group in your area that you can go to. At first one-year-olds only play side by side. It is at about eighteen months that they start to interact in play. Now the concept of sharing has to be introduced, and until it has been accepted there will be conflicts over toys (and probably afterwards as well!). This is the time to present the idea of fairness, and the notion of being considerate to others for social reasons (not because you'll be punished if you don't). By the age of two playing with little friends will be something your child will look forward to and enjoy. Having friends home to play and paying return visits is the backbone of social activity in childhood and can be very rewarding for parents too, who can feel isolated if they spend too much time alone at home.

Standard clinic tests
Either at eighteen months or two years you will be asked to take your baby to the child health clinic for a check on development. You will be seen by the health visitor or doctor or possibly both (see page 15). As well as checking on your child's weight and height, vision and hearing tests will be given, and the ears and teeth will be inspected. In order to assess the progress of your child's overall development, he or she will be asked to perform a few simple tasks, such as building a tower of bricks, and by talking to your child the health visitor will be able to gauge the level of alertness and understanding. Many children are inhibited by the occasion and seem unable to do things you know they are quite capable of doing at home. The health visitor understands this and will take it into account when making the assessment.

Pre-school child: two to five years
Care of the teeth

By 18 months your child should be encouraged to brush the teeth after every meal and certainly before going to bed. Your child can visit the dentist for a check-up at around two years and at six-month intervals thereafter. All the milk teeth should have appeared by two years, calling for careful brushing to remove all specks of food that may be stuck between them. If your child eats sweets remember that the most harmful are sticky sweets and those that stay in the mouth for a long time. Rinsing out with water will help cleanse the mouth until a time when the teeth can be properly brushed.

Cognitive development through play

The importance of play in a child's development cannot

Play

• Concepts of opposites are understood at this stage - that Mummy and Daddy are big but he or she is small; the bathwater is hot but an ice-cream is cold.

• Sorting games encourage awareness of shape and color. A child can complete jigsaws with large pieces and simple designs, matching up the shapes and holding the concept of a finished picture to aim for in the mind.

• Looking at a book is an intellectual and physical learning activity requiring the ability to hold the book, turn the pages in the right order and focus on the page. When you read a story to your child, sit him or her comfortably on your lap so that your child can see the image on the paper and help to turn the pages.

• The powers of concentration and memory are improving all the time: your child will be delighted on a visit to the zoo to recognize the animals that were in a story the night before.

• Being able to listen is an important feature of learning which is enhanced by story-reading and story-telling. Some excellent taped recordings of children's stories are now available which your child will enjoy.

be overstated. Playing with other children, while building up confidence, is often adventurous and energetic as well as sociable, but remember that a child can also happily occupy himself or herself for half an hour. Both contribute to intellectual development, particularly if the playthings you provide are chosen to satisfy the needs of growing capabilities.

Children of both sexes like playing with cuddly toys, and later with dolls. Playing with dolls gives children the opportunity to make a world in miniature which they can control and understand, helping them to act out the challenges of real life and make sense of them.

The primary school child
From five to eleven

During the primary school years (and beyond) your child should continue to grow at a steady rate. If you have kept weight and height charts since babyhood you will know where your child fits with regard to the 'average' line of development and how regular the growth rate has been. You can continue to keep a record of gains in weight and height - every three months is often enough - to see that the rate of growth continues as it should. A child may temporaily put on some extra weight after a period of overeating, say on summer holidays with snacks and ice-creams, then right itself. Similarly weight loss after illness will be regained, as normally babies and children 'catch up' very quickly.

Cognitive development

By the time they go to school at five years of age, most children are ready to start learning to read and write and grasp some basic mathematical concepts. In fact they will very likely have started to do all these things already, but in a less formally organized way than in the classroom. Many will have learnt to recognize some words, probably their own name and one or two items from an alphabet picture book. While few children will write competently, those who have had plenty of opportunity to draw and paint at home will know how to hold a pencil and to make the curved and straight lines that make up the Roman alphabet. Tracing drawings helps children to control their hands and contributes to first steps in writing. In mathematics and science knowledge of different shapes and colors can be built on to enhance the concept of numbers, of more and less, longer and shorter, heavier and lighter. All these ideas are carried through the curriculum in work on projects like the weather which can be explored in painting and writing as well as measuring and comparing.

In the primary school environment children meet the first and most demanding social task of their lives: to achieve a degree of independence from home while forming relationships with strangers strong enough to withstand the strains of everyday ups-and-downs. The comforting regularity of the school day gives a strong framework in which this adventure can be played out, and with the love and support of their parents the overwhelming majority of children make a great success of it.

At five years, the average weight for girls is 19.5 kg (41 lb) and height 1m 6 cm (3ft 6 in): for boys weight is very slightly less and height fractionally more. By the age of eleven, the difference between the sexes is still minimal, and both boys and girls will on average weigh 34 kg (75 lb) and be 1.42 m (4 ft 8 in) in height.

Healthy development

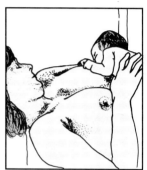

In late pregnancy some antibodies are transferred from you to your baby via the placenta, affording protection in the first few months against viral infections such as chickenpox. After birth, the colostrum produced by the breasts before the milk comes in is rich in antibodies giving your baby a further degree of immunity. Even if you can only breastfeed for a week or two you will have given your baby an excellent start in life.

Health in pregnancy

Most pregnant women have few problems, as distinct from discomforts such as heartburn or breathlessness which are certainly a nuisance but not harmful. Keeping healthy in pregnancy is sensible for mothers as well as their babies. In the absence of circumstances such as diabetes which need special care, the management of pregnancy is a matter of common sense. Pregnancy makes you tired, for example, and when you're tired you should rest, even if it means leaving some work undone. Ideally, give up going out to work when you feel ready.

While pregnancy is not a sickness, regular antenatal visits to the hospital clinic or your doctor are important. Checks on your weight are important for you, but also give an indication that your baby is growing properly. Blood pressure is regularly checked, as hypertension (high blood pressure) can lead to problems in labor if untreated. There are a number of special antenatal tests which are now available. Blood tests reveal inherited blood disorders that can cause disability. At about 15 weeks, a test to measure alpha feto protein (AFP) levels in the blood is done. High AFP levels can indicate spina bifida and will require further investigation. Ultrasound scans are routine in pregnancy to check the position and development of the fetus and the position of the placenta. In amniocentesis a sample of the amniotic fluid is drawn off from the uterus and analyzed to check for chromosomal abnormalities such as Down's syndrome. These and other checks carried out in the antenatal period are designed to identify possible complications and ensure that you have a safe delivery.

Newborn health

Resistance to infection

Newborn babies are resilient creatures. Nevertheless they are vulnerable to infection after leaving the protection of the uterus, and are not yet strong enough to deal with it. While you can take care to keep infection at bay by observing strict hygiene and keeping people with colds at a distance, it is also important to build up your baby's resistance to infection.

Early feeding
The rigid four-hourly-feed system of a generation ago has given way to a more relaxed method of feeding babies when they are hungry. This is often called 'demand feeding', and although it may be time consuming in the early days when babies need to be fed a little and often, they soon settle down to a regular pattern. Most mothers find that feeding babies when they cry is far less stressful than carrying them around and trying to comfort them until the 'correct' time of day for the next feed is reached. The baby may just need the comfort of sucking and your close embrace, and will settle down to sleep again after only a short feed.

Breastfeeding
Breast milk is ideally suited to a new baby, as it is composed of exactly the right proportion of protein, carbohydrate, fat and iron and is very low in sodium (salt). The advantages of breastfeeding are primarily that breast milk is the perfect food for your baby and that it contains antibodies which are of enormous benefit in building up his or her resistance to infection. The colostrum or 'pre-milk' which the breasts produce immediately after birth and for the first day or two is particularly rich in these antibodies.

Many mothers are further encouraged to breastfeed if there are problems of allergy in the family, such as hay fever, asthma and eczema, but there is no hard evidence that breastfeeding protects against allergy. However, some babies are allergic to cow's milk protein which is used in the majority of formula feeds.

Breastfeeding is also hygienic, convenient in the sense that you can do it anywhere and any time, and, not a small consideration, totally free! You do not need to 'eat for two' when breastfeeding any more than you did when pregnant, because most of the calories you need have been stored up in pregnancy. Having said that, a good

Winding
Both breastfed and bottle-fed babies sometimes need winding. When they bring up wind, babies usually bring up a little milk with it, so have a cloth at the ready. Place your baby against your shoulder, or on your lap, chin supported by your finger and thumb, and rub or pat your baby gently in the center of the back. Don't overdo this or the whole feed may come back up. If you don't get a burp after a few minutes, stop.

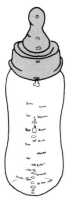

The conventional rigid bottle made of clear plastic with a measure printed on the side. These bottles and the teats used with them must be sterilized before use every time. When feeding, the teat has to be released from the mouth every so often to let air into the bottle to equalize the pressure and allow the baby to go on sucking.

balanced diet with enough protein is essential. If you are anemic your doctor will prescribe iron tablets for a while. Other medication may have to be modified because certain drugs can appear in the breast milk.

You should be comfortable when breastfeeding: sit well supported with a pillow under the arm supporting your baby. Your midwife or health visitor will be available to help with any difficulties in the first few weeks. Don't worry about quantities because you cannot see how much milk your baby is getting. In the very early days feeding 'on demand' satisfies the baby and stimulates the breasts to go on producing milk. Soon a pattern of six or seven feeds a day will establish itself. If the baby sucks for eight minutes or so on each side he or she will be well nourished. Offer both breasts at each feed, alternating the breast you offer first so that production of milk is even. Keep a glass of water to hand because it is quite common to feel intensely thirsty as the milk 'lets down' at the start of the feed.

The so-called disadvantages of breastfeeding are more to do with attitudes held by some women which lead them to regard the process with distaste. There is no truth in the myth that breastfeeding spoils a woman's figure: it has no permanent effect on the shape of the breasts, and actually helps to get the uterus back into shape after birth. Breastfeeding does restrict the length of time a mother can be away from the baby, unless milk is expressed into a (sterilized) bottle so that the father or a friend can feed the baby occasionally.

Bottle-feeding
Bottle-feeding calls for more practical planning than breastfeeding, from choosing and buying bottles, teats and sterilizing equipment to actually making up the feeds for your baby's daily needs. Bottle-feeding gives the mother a degree of freedom as other people can feed the baby if she has to be away from home for any period, particularly if she returns to work. It is important to cuddle your baby when bottle-feeding just as you would if he or she were at the breast. Your baby needs not only

the milk in the bottle, but also the physical warmth and closeness.

Equipment for bottle-feeding

Different bottles need different teats. Make sure the hole in the teat is large enough to release a steady stream of drips from the bottle when it is held upside down.

Bottles, teats, caps and covers must be thoroughly sterilized before use. The old-fashioned method is to place them in boiling water for five minutes, drain off the water and leave them covered, preferably in the refrigerator, until required. The modern method is to submerge all feeding equipment in a sterilizing solution for a given period. The solution is made by dissolving a concentrated liquid or tablet in water. A plastic sterilizing unit to contain the feeding equipment in the solution is not essential but extremely useful. The unit has an inner cover to keep the bottles and teats submerged in the liquid with no air bubbles and an outer cover to seal it. Use a fresh solution every day. When you need the bottles and teats, remove them carefully by the outside edges. Shake off the excess liquid but do not rinse the bottles. Do not dry them with a cloth or put them down to drain. Fill them with milk and seal them straight away.

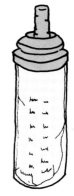

This type of feeder is not a bottle but a polythene bag mounted on a plastic holder which is covered with a teat. These bags, which can only be used once, are already sterile so only the teats and tops need to be sterilized. The bag collapses as the baby sucks, so there is no vacuum as in a conventional bottle and your baby can suck without stopping.

Making up feeds

Formulas for bottle-feeding are usually based on cow's milk, specially treated to make it resemble human milk as closely as possible. There are different formulas available. Your midwife or health visitor will advise you on the best choice for your baby. Because of the care with which formula feeds are made, it is essential that you make them up exactly as instructed by the manufacturer. Packets include a scoop measure so that you can be sure you use the right amount. Do not be tempted to make the formula richer by increasing the proportion of milk powder to water. This can be dangerous for your baby as it increases the sodium content of the feed. Do not use the scoop provided with one brand of formula for another.

Make up a full day's supply of milk at a time and

Domestic hygiene

With a baby in the house, you will almost certainly be so busy that housework is kept at a minimum. With time only for the essentials, let the kitchen, bathroom and lavatory take priority. Keep the rest of the house as tidy as you can and when you have time to dust and vacuum-clean it will be much easier. Keep clothes and bedclothes laundered, using laundry services when you can to save time and energy. If you have cats or dogs you must be extra watchful to keep them clean, free of fleas and away from the baby.

keep the filled bottles in the refrigerator. For the night feeds it is particularly useful to have a bottle ready. Boil a kettleful of water. Wash your hands carefully. Remove the bottles from the sterilizing solution as described above and place them on a flat surface. Pour the required amount of hot water into the bottles. Using the scoop provided, add the required number of scoops of powder to each bottle. The scoop should be level: do not press the powder down, but level it off with the blade of a knife. Put in the teats upside down, cover the bottles immediately and shake them well to dissolve the powder. When they have cooled, place them in the refrigerator until needed. If you need a bottle fairly soon, let it cool down at least to blood temperature: a few drops on the back of your hand should feel neither hot nor cold. For later feeds, there is no real need to warm the bottles, though some people like to. If your baby likes cold milk, you can be confident it is not harmful.

If your baby does not finish a bottle at a single feed, throw away the milk that remains. If you have any bottles left from a single day's batch, throw the milk away and start afresh for the next 24-hour period.

Quantity of feeds

A newborn baby of average weight will probably take about 575 ml (just over 1 pint) in the course of a day, though not necessarily equal amounts at each feed. At seven days he or she may be taking 90 ml (3 fl oz) at each feed. This will increase slowly but steadily until at three months you can expect to be giving five feeds per day of 250 ml (8 fl oz) each, that is, a full bottle.

Food hygiene

It is essential to observe rules of hygiene when preparing food under any circumstances, but especially when the food is for your baby. In the first six months, when the immune system is immature, babies are most vulnerable to infection. A simple and vital precaution is to wash your hands well before preparing food or eating. If you are bottle-feeding, keep all equipment sterile as described above. After a feed, wash out and rinse the bottle and leave it to drain until you make up the next batch of sterilizing solution. Rub the teats with salt to remove milk deposits and rinse well. If you give your baby water to drink, use a sterilized bottle and teat and water which has been boiled in the kettle and allowed to cool. Bottled mineral water is not sterile and some brands contain a lot of salt.

The greatest danger to your baby's health is posed by warm milk, which is an ideal breeding-ground for bacteria. Milk that has been left to stand and get warm can give your baby gastroenteritis severe enough to mean admission to hospital. When you have made up the day's feeds, cool the bottles as soon as you can by putting them in the refrigerator and be ruthless about throwing away milk left in bottles. If you are away from home for a day and have to take a bottle or two with you, transfer them from the refrigerator to an insulated picnic box which will keep them cold until required.

When your baby starts on solid food, keep dishes and spoons perfectly clean by washing them in hot soapy water, rinsing in hot water and leaving to drain. Tea towels are host to legions of germs and should not be used. A teacher beaker should be sterilized as milk deposits can lodge in the spout. Dummies (pacifiers) are almost impossible to keep clean, which is one reason for not using them. If you must, sterilize them as often as possible. Tins and jars of commercially prepared purées contain much more food than your baby wants at one meal, but you cannot give use the left-overs later. Dehydrated foods enable you to make up tiny amounts at a time without waste. When you do use tins, keep an opener specially for your baby's foods and scald the top of the can with boiling water before opening it. Do not use the same chopping board for raw meat and other food: keep one just for that purpose. Keep all kitchen surfaces immaculately clean.

Bathing your baby

Some new babies dislike being placed naked in a bath of

Bathing

Assemble everything you need first: towels, soap or bath liquid, cotton wool, tissues, baby lotion or oil if needed, and a clean nappy and clothes. Wear a towelling apron or wrap a towel round your waist. Have the room warm: your baby should not feel cold at any time. A baby bath on a stand makes the job easier. The kitchen sink will do, but take care with the taps. Fill the bath with warm water, testing the temperature with your elbow. Add bath liquid if using and swish it round. Undress your baby and clean the bottom with a tissue or wad of damp cotton wool. Wrap the baby in a towel and sit him or her on your lap to wash the face with cotton wool. Do not use a face flannel as these are very unhygienic. Hold the head over the bath to rinse the scalp and pat it dry. Unwrap the towel, leaving it on your lap, and lower your baby into the water, supporting neck and head with one hand, bottom with the other. Hold like this until the baby is relaxed, then take one hand away and wash him or her all over. Allow play for a bit before lifting the baby out on to the towel and wrapping up snugly to dry. Make sure all the creases are dry. Powder in damp groins and armpits cakes, creating an irritating lump.

Disposable nappies

The overwhelming advantage of disposable nappies is that they dispense with the need for buckets of sterilant and extra laundry. They are very easy to put on, with strips of adhesive tape to fix them at each side instead of safety pins. If you tear the strips, masking tape can be used instead. Of the various designs available, the all-in-one type incorporating nappy liner, absorbent pad and plastic pants is best, and those with elasticated legs have the best fit: they look neat and don't leak. For night-time, you can put an extra pad inside the nappy with a nappy liner. As disposables can only be used once, it's important always to have plenty in store. Even if you use terry-towelling nappies most of the time, a box of disposable nappies is handy for emergencies and very useful when traveling. Disposable nappies will almost certainly block the loo if you try to flush them away. It's best to dispose of feces in the lavatory and place the nappies themselves in a plastic sack tied firmly at the neck.

water. For them it is adequate to make sure hands, face and bottom are washed regularly with pads of cotton wool and warm water. Eventually all babies have the confidence to go in the bath if you take it gently. Topping and tailing is a daily necessity but giving your baby a bath can be a very pleasant prelude to bedtime.

Nappy-changing routines

You will probably have decided early on whether to use terry-towelling nappies or disposables. In practice a combination of the two works well, if you have the facilities for washing terry nappies. Since terry-towelling nappies are so absorbent they are particularly useful at night, while disposables are neat and easy for daytime use.

Changing a nappy

Put your baby on the mat and remove the dirty nappy. Use cotton wool dampened with warm water to remove urine. For a boy, wipe from the legs inwards, without pulling back the foreskin. For a girl, do not pull back the labia to clean inside, and wipe from the vagina towards the anus to prevent the spread of bacteria. Dry gently but thoroughly with tissues. If the nappy is soiled, use the front to wipe away the worst of the feces. Fold it over and place it to one side while you clean the baby. Use cotton wool and lotion or oil to wipe the baby's bottom completely clean. Apply nappy rash cream if necessary before putting on a clean nappy.

Lay the folded nappy on a safe flat surface. Place a nappy liner in the center and have safety pins to hand. Place your baby down with the widest part of the nappy at the waist. Draw the front fold up between the legs and hold it in place while you bring up the two side folds (see page 38 for a variety of folds). Fasten and close the pins. Put a clean pair of plastic pants on top and dress your baby again. Dispose of the dirty nappy and wash your hands.

Sterilizing nappies

Fabric nappies must be sterilized to clean them of traces

of ammonia and bacteria that could cause irritation or infection. Sterilizing powder dissolved in water cleans them thoroughly without the need for boiling. Prepare sterilizing liquid in two lidded buckets, one for wet nappies and one for those that are soiled. Put enough water in the buckets and add the sterilizing powder. Make a fresh batch every day. Wet nappies should be rinsed out in cold water, wrung out and immersed in sterilizing liquid for the recommended time. When the nappy is soiled, dispose of the feces in the lavatory (a nappy liner makes this easier and can be flushed away), rinse the nappy and place it in the appropriate bucket.

Nappies that were wet need only be thoroughly rinsed in hot water to remove the sterilizing solution before being dried. Soiled nappies should be washed in hot soapy water and rinsed. Fabric conditioner is not necessary and may cause nappy rash. Nappies dried in the open air or a tumble drier stay soft; placed on radiators to dry, the fabric will harden. Wash plastic pants in warm soapy water, pat them dry and allow them to air before use. Tumble drying will make the plastic brittle.

Parent-child bonding

A bond of love between a child and a parent is essential for complete development, not just of an emotional nature, but of intellectual and physical powers as well. Children who are deprived of this love are solitary and introverted, and later may be aggressive and unable to make friends. This parent-child bond begins to be forged almost immediately after birth, when the newborn baby fixes his or her gaze on the mother's eyes, and is intensified if put to the breast and suckled straight away. This stimulates hormones in the mother's brain that actually increases her feelings of tenderness. Physical warmth and contact between a baby and the mother and father makes the bond that joins them stronger day by day. Carrying your baby in a sling is the best way of keeping him or her close to you, hearing your heart beat and sensing your movements just as in the womb. Eye-to-eye contact with your baby is vital, as is the sound of your

Terry-towelling nappies
You will need at least 24 fabric nappies. This represents a high initial cost, but works out cheaper eventually if you keep them to use for second and subsequent babies. The basic nappy is a terry-towelling square; shaped nappies do not need folding to fit, but are less efficient. Muslin nappies are soft, thin squares for new babies, but need changing frequently. As well as the nappies you will need nappy liners to keep your baby dry, safety pins with covered ends and plastic pants.

When changing a nappy you will need:
• changing mat
• clean terry-towelling nappy with liner, pins and plastic pants or
• disposable nappy
• tissues
• cotton wool
• bowl of warm water
• baby lotion or oil
• nappy rash cream

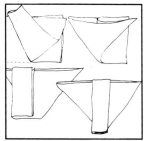

This nappy fold is the neatest and most useful when your baby is tiny.

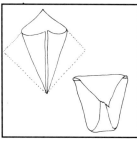

This also gives a neat finish when the baby is larger and can be adjusted as he or she grows.

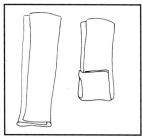

This is somewhat bulky but is good for boys or girls who sleep on their tummies as the most absorbent panel is at the front.

voice: speak gently and rhythmically. Your presence gives the reassurance needed. You represent security, and on that foundation your baby is most likely to flourish.

Toys in stimulating development
At different stages of development, different toys are suitable for satisfying your baby's curiosity and exercising new skills. In this early period, before your child is able to sit, toys that he or she can hold and shake to produce different sounds are also of great interest. Your child also needs things to watch, such as mobiles and a string of toys across cot or pram. Remember that any object used as a toy is a tool of learning too. A baby or child who is bored and neglected will not be motivated to develop skills such as body control, concentration and the quest for knowledge: playthings that give pleasure are crucial in stimulating that motivation.

Immunization programme
You will be asked to bring your baby to the child health clinic for the first round of his vaccinations at about three months old. It is important for the health of the whole community that you have your child immunized. Pertussis (whooping cough), diphtheria, tetanus and poliomyelitis are serious diseases which are now far less common because of the immunization programme. The 'triple' vaccine, DTP, protects against diphtheria, tetanus and pertussis and is given by injection (as is the MMR vaccine later, see page 45). You can choose to have your child immunized against the first two only. The second DTP vaccine is given at five to six months. On both occasions your baby will be given polio vaccine by mouth. The third dose of DTP and polio vaccine is given between nine and eleven months.

Healthy six months to one year
Introduction of mixed feeding
Your baby will probably start mixed feeding at about four

VITAMINS		
A	For healthy bone development	Milk, butter, egg yolk, fatty fish, cod liver oil
B GROUP	For red blood cell formation, maintenance of nervous tissue	Pulses, wholemeal bread, raw carrots, cabbage, yeast, liver, fish
C	For clear skin, strong gums, teeth and bones	All fruit especially citrus; all vegetables especially green and red peppers
D	For sound teeth and bones	Milk, butter, cheese, fatty fish. Made by body in sunlight.

Vitamins A, C and D can be given to your baby in the form of drops until he or she is eating a wider mixed diet that satisfies the vitamin requirements. Vitamin C must be taken every day as it cannot be stored in the body. It is partially destroyed by cooking: serve fruit and vegetables lightly cooked or raw if possible.

MINERALS		
CALCIUM	For strong bones and teeth; muscle formation	Dairy foods; eggs, flour, bread, oatmeal, green vegetables, tinned sardines (with bones)
IRON	Enables body to use essential oxygen	Liver, kidneys, meat, egg yolk, potatoes, cabbage, water, raisins

Sodium, potassium and phosphorus are also necessary but are present in many foods and a deficiency is unlikely.

• **Protein** is essential for maintaining growth. Good sources are meat, fish, cheese, eggs, peas, lentils, beans and wheat.

• **Carbohydrates** give energy and help the digestion of fats. Children need a certain amount of carbohydrate to replenish their energy, but an excess will lead to overweight and carbohydrates derived from starchy foods such as potatoes, rice and bread are much better than those in sugary foods which damage the teeth, spoil a baby's taste buds and are low in nutrients.

• **Fats** are concentrated forms of energy foods that also help to keep us warm. They are essential in the diet but in small quantities. Sources are fat meat, butter, cream, margarine and oils. Vitamins ensure normal growth and health. The most important are listed below

• **Fiber** is necessary for healthy bowel function and is present in green vegetables, salads, wholemeal bread and fruit.

At six months a bottle-fed baby can change to ordinary cow's milk, which should be boiled and cooled. Breastfed babies can also be weaned on to cow's milk. Offer it in a teacher beaker, rather than introducing a bottle to a baby who has never used one.

months, certainly by six months since at this point he or she will need more iron in the diet than is provided by breast milk or cow's milk alone. A balanced diet includes foods containing protein, carbohydrate, fats, vitamins and minerals plus fiber and water.

Choice of solid foods
What you give your baby in a mixed diet will be dictated by all the nutrients that are needed for healthy development which can only be acquired from variety in the diet.

Most babies' first taste of solid food is a teaspoon of ready-prepared cereal such as rice. These are excellent, easy to digest and much more nutritious than the cereals sold for adult consumption. The nutritional difference between other commercially prepared foods and those you make yourself is less marked, though you are more in control of the child's diet if you produce freshly cooked home-made meals. Cans and jars of food are more convenient to use as they involve no preparation and can be served anywhere. Their nutritional value is consistent; home-made meals will vary according to the method of preparation and speed of serving. Your own food has lots of variety and can be adapted to suit an individual's taste, whereas a canned lamb hotpot always looks and tastes the same. A baby who has been given puréed versions of ordinary family meals is more likely to enjoy what everyone else is eating as he or she gets older.

In practice a largely home-prepared diet with a proportion of canned foods for convenience will work out well. If you depend heavily on commercially prepared foods, add fresh finger foods such as cubes of cheese and grated vegetables to the menu. Never add salt or sugar to your baby's food.

Emotional development
In the second half of the first year your relationship with your baby continues to grow, and your position as the central figure in his or her life is confirmed. The child's devotion for you is demonstrated in smiles and gurgles and what can sometimes feel like an insatiable demand

for cuddles and attention. It often happens at this stage that babies become fearful of being separated from their mothers. It is important not to deepen anxiety by belittling his or her distress when parted from you. Reassure him or her by keeping separations to a minimum, and always leave your child with a familiar person. Reinforce the trust in you now so that confidence can grow naturally as the social circle widens.

A baby or child who is secure is free to explore life and develop physically, mentally and emotionally. Your baby does not simply enjoy your company when you play together, but also learns from you the things the world has to offer, ducks on the pond, sand on the beach, the sound of the piano keys, and your child grows with every new experience.

Toddler health

Dietary needs

Many parents are concerned that their active toddler, ever on the move and choosy about foods, is being undernourished. But children don't starve themselves as long as they are offered enough food. Even if your 18-month-old eats nothing but bread, apples and milk for a fortnight no harm will come of it, since these three items are between them providing all the elements necessary in a balanced diet, even if it is rather monotonous. If your child is happy on a conventional mixed diet, that's fine. Even if not, however, you can reassure yourself he or she is getting all the necessary nutrients by looking at the foods that are enjoyed: the chances are that these favorites incorporate enough protein, carbohydrate and fat to maintain health, especially if milk is still drunk. Continue to give vitamin drops if you are worried, but resist the temptation to entice him or her with sweets, biscuits and cakes. Above all, don't force a child to eat. It is not necessary and can turn mealtimes into a long-term battlefield.

To be overweight at any stage is a health hazard. It is inhibiting for toddlers, as it takes longer to achieve

Oral hygiene

Even if it is not always possible for your child to brush the teeth after eating sweets, this must be done last thing at night (or after anything, even a milky drink) and after breakfast in the morning. Use a small soft toothbrush and make sure all the teeth are cleaned. Get your child into the habit of rinsing out the mouth with water after meals if it is not convenient to brush the teeth.

Ask your dentist if the local water supply is fluorinated and if not, whether fluoride tablets are recommended for your child. Make sure your child's diet includes enough calcium and vitamin D, which promote strong teeth and bones.

Before your child is two, a visit to the dentist is advisable, even if no treatment is necessary. Early visits to check dental development and health can save many problems later and it is best to build up your child's confidence in the dentist before any treatment is needed.

coordination with a bulky body. A fat, as opposed to a naturally big, toddler will have rings of fat on the thighs and upper arms. Never put your child on a slimming diet to counteract a tendency to fat. A child should not lose weight, but slow down the rate of weight gain. Reduce the proportion of calories coming from fats, sweets, sweet snacks and sweetened drinks. Substitute boiled potatoes for chips, fresh and dried fruit for snacks, and water biscuits for cakes.

There is no doubt that sweets are harmful. With management you may be able to keep them out of the picture for the first year or two, even longer, but sooner or later you will have to formulate a workable policy on rationing. This might be one sweet a day, two every evening, or Saturdays only, whatever suits you. Restrict them to after a meal when the mouth is being washed with more saliva than usual. Try to get your child into a habit of tooth cleaning after eating sweet things such as ice-creams and sweetened drinks as well as sweets and chocolates.

Opinions are divided about the use of sweets as treats and rewards: certainly there is no reason why your child should not be encouraged to think of a fresh peach as a treat instead of a lollipop.

Sleep problems

In the toddler period, your child will probably sleep slightly less at night. While daytime naps are still needed, their duration is awkward to manage. Two long naps are too much, making it difficult to settle down at night, and one may not be enough. It may be necessary to wake your child from an afternoon sleep if it threatens to push back bedtime too far. Until a child is able to get through a busy day with one nap, help with the tired patches by organizing quiet periods when you sit and play or read together. A toddler's life is exciting and demanding, and he or she will go on playing until too exhausted to relax at bedtime. When you can see that a game is getting too much, offer a more restful diversion before it's gone too far.

Problems in going to sleep at night are very common

at this period. If overtiredness is the cause, your child may need an extra rest during the day. Even then, at least half of all children of this age resist going to sleep. It is much easier to handle if you have an existing bedtime routine. Even if such routines don't come naturally to you, it may be worth making the effort to introduce one now in the interests of getting your own dinner on the table and eating it in peace. Once your child has been put to bed, warm, bathed and story over, the important thing is that he or she stays there. Don't leave your child alone to cry in misery, but don't pick him or her up either - pop your head round the door to show you haven't forgotten, but then go away again. You may have to do this several times, but it's better than taking the child back to disrupt your evening completely.

Cognitive development

To help your toddler as he or she energetically explores the world, let him or her play with water, make some play-dough and go to the sandpit, so that he or she can experiment with these substances and discover their properties. Provide toys that exploit hand-and-eye coordination and exercise the need to know how things fit together; shape-sorters, stacking beakers, a set of colored bricks. While children need to find a place in the real world by helping to wash the car or sweep the floor, they need to make personal worlds too, with a toy farmyard or a doll's house. Imagination is beginning to flower: a dressing-up box full of assorted old clothes is a great spur to invention.

Give your child the opportunity to be with other children now as a basis for the interactive play which follows. While they may not communicate with each other yet, toddlers are eager to talk to their parents, and delight in encouragement. The interesting vocabulary you offer them is vital information in the language-building process. Adults often communicate with each other in a shorthand of gestures and words: children need you to be much more theatrical, acting out what you are saying so the message comes over loud and clear.

Flexible shoes that bend easily with the foot encourage a natural springy step. All shoes should be supple, especially where the toe joints bend, but firm in the arch. Shoes with laces or an adjustable strap are best because they hold the foot firmly to the back of the shoe and prevent it from sliding forward and cramping the toes. Fit shoes while the child is standing up because feet should always be measured while weight-bearing. The growing foot must be checked regularly to see how much it has increased in size and whether the shoe is still large enough. If shoes are bought with a growing space of 18 mm (3/4 inch) at the toe they are likely to last as long as it takes the foot to grow and use up the spare space.

Care of the feet

Shoes are not necessary for babies until they begin to walk unaided. Even then, let your child go barefoot whenever possible, or in socks that are not too tight. The tremendous flexibility of infants' feet is important in finding balance and is a key factor in healthy feet throughout life.

Feet should be washed as part of the daily bathing routine, using ordinary toilet soap and water. If there is much sweating use baby powder between the toes and make sure that clean socks are put on every day. Toe-nails should be trimmed regularly. They should not be cut too short, but should rest on the pulp at the end of the toe. The corners of nails should never be cut out, nor should a sharp instrument ever be used to clean the sides of the nail. If dirt collects down the side of a nail, it may be cleaned out using a soft brush.

Clean socks every day help to keep the skin healthy. Shrunk socks can cause a child's soft bones to grow crooked. All socks or tights should be long enough to pull away leaving room to spare at the toe ends. When socks are washed they should be pulled out and stretched into shape.

Healthy pre-school year

Diet and nutrition

Many pre-school children have amazingly healthy and unfussy appetites, though not all. As in the toddler stage, however, children who are offered adequate nutrition will not let themselves starve. Children may have a passion for tomato sandwiches one week and macaroni cheese the next, to the virtual exclusion of all else. In the long term these extremes balance out and provide adequate nutrients. If your child is drinking a pint of milk daily and taking vitamin drops to supplement the diet, however meagre it may seem some days, this is fine. If you have any worries about weight gain, ask your doctor or health visitor.

You can now offer your child anything that the rest

44

of the family is eating, even spicy dishes. Along with a more adult diet, your child is ready to join in with mealtimes as a social event and to learn the conventions of more formal meals. Impeccable table manners cannot be acquired overnight, but improve gradually, by your example and encouragement, because children are motivated to be with you and gain your approval for their behavior. Let them join in the preparation of the meal by helping you lay the table attractively, and give them proper cutlery to use (child-sized) instead of plastic spoons. High chairs cut children off from everyone else; but on ordinary chairs with a booster seat for the smaller ones, they are better able to join in the general conversation.

Immunization program

At about fifteen months, though it can be delayed if necessary, your child should be given the MMR vaccine. This protects against measles, mumps and rubella, three diseases which can cause great suffering and long-term damage. Some children develop a mild fever and rash a week to ten days after being immunized, but this subsides within three days and is not infectious.

At the age of five, the booster shots for diphtheria and tetanus are given, plus the oral vaccine for polio. A note for the future: further boosters for both tetanus and polio should be given when your teenage child leaves school and again later in adulthood (that means you, too). This is particularly important in the case of polio. A few parents, more often the fathers, get polio following the immunization of their children.

First steps to independence

By the time your child is in the third year, trust in you is firmly rooted. He or she has begun to make strong attachments with others, too, such as grandparents or a regular babysitter, and to enjoy the company of peers. While you want to encourage independence, be patient and remember that he or she still needs frequent demonstrations of love from you to sustain that precious sense of security.

Faddy feeders

Forcing a child to eat something he or she dislikes is unreasonable, and can make a child resistant to all food. Respect personal tastes as you would those of an adult, once you know what they are - don't think of them as 'fads'. If you are worried that the tastes leave him or her short of particularly nourishing foods, eggs, for example, serve them disguised as pancakes and avoid a showdown. Don't insist that a child always finishes everything on the plate: the child knows his or her own capacity.

Part of social awareness is respecting the needs of others. At mealtimes this means that your child should not be permitted to spoil things for others at the table, by taking all the 'best' bits of a pudding, for example. If you have presented a meal which you know he or she likes and yet refuses, don't cajole him by giving him or her something different. Let your child choose to eat what he or she can or go without.

Preschool care
• Private nursery schools have a distinctly educational bias, consciously preparing their pupils for the intellectual and social demands of school. They usually keep school hours, opening in term-time only.
• Day nurseries are open all day, all year, since their main purpose is to ensure parents go out to work. Since they are responsible for the children for such a great part of the day, concern for their physical welfare is as important a consideration as developing individual skills. Even if you do not go out to work, you may feel that your child would benefit from the various activities of a playgroup or kindergarten and would enjoy the company; but don't send your child until ready. A very shy child will become more introverted if forced into the hurly-burly too soon.

Learning acceptable group behavior is something you can help with by observing your child at play. He or she may get along swimmingly and instinctively take turns on the swing and share toys. On the other hand, you may need to teach that cooperation with the others means everyone has more fun. If this lesson is not learnt before going to school, the first term could be very difficult. Having friends home to play will reinforce a child's sense of belonging on his or her own territory and increase pride in the home. It's up to you to issue the invitations!

Part of independence is taking responsibility for yourself, and there are many ways in which you can encourage your child to do this. The phase of encouraging children to clean their teeth, put their clothes in the laundry basket or their toys in the cupboard may seem to last indefinitely but eventually children do develop good habits and living sociably alongside the rest of the family becomes second nature.

Children of this age know what they like to wear. You can encourage them to stick to clothes which are comfortable and easy to do up and put on, but their peer group will influence the colors and style. At this age you must adopt a guiding role, not a controlling one. When children feel they have made the right choices for themselves, they have the self-confidence needed to cope with school.

Healthy primary school years
Diet and nutrition
Between the ages of seven and ten a child needs 2,400 calories a day. This is the most a girl will need at any time in her life except when pregnant or breastfeeding. For a boy, the figure continues to rise until his early twenties, when it begins to decline.

A large proportion of the primary school child's energy needs should come from nutritious foods, that is those rich in protein and which satisfy the requirement for carbohydrate, fat and vitamins. Because meat, fish, eggs and cheese are very concentrated forms of protein, relatively small amounts are highly nutritious; but hamburgers, sausages and fish fingers contain protein as well, and if your child likes them there is no harm in letting him or her have them. Potatoes and bread fulfil an important role in a healthy diet, since they are satisfying foods which provide energy, protein and vitamins.

If your child's basic diet is sound, don't worry too much if what we think of as 'junk' food is occasionally enjoyed, attractively packaged items loaded with additives. If such foods were eaten to the exclusion of all else, that would certainly be damaging, but eating them in moderation won't do any harm and is not worth having a battle over. If your family diet is based on fresh nutritious foods and if, as your child gets older, you teach what is good to eat, your child's own tastes and preferences will probably tend towards the healthy.

Many parents feel that their child should have a good breakfast before school, but the child may not agree. Point out that he or she will be ravenous by mid-morning but don't force your child to eat a huge spread. A glass of milk and a biscuit will do, especially if you provide an apple to silence the mid-morning pangs. Packeted cereals are very convenient and most children should be able to find something they like from the huge range on offer. Wholemeal toast and fruit juice is a good combination. If you have a little extra time (make the batter the night before), pancakes are nutritious and popular.

If your child's school offers good lunches, make use of them. You may prefer to make your own packed lunches, however. There is no point in putting together a menu that your child won't eat. Make a list of lunches that you think are suitable and agree with your child on a set of five so that something different can be had every day, giving some power of choice. Original it may not be, but sandwiches made with good fresh bread are an excellent basis for lunch. Suitable fillings include cheese, egg, ham and cold chicken, perhaps with tomato slices. Other ideas are a piece of cheese with a celery stalk and a sandwich. Older children might like a chicken drumstick with a bread roll. Individually wrapped salami sausages are popular; ration them as they are high in salt. Potato crisps contain protein - but choose the low-fat kind. Yogurt is protein-rich, makes a good 'pudding' and is easy to pack. Include a carton of real fruit juice, a piece of fruit and perhaps a small muesli bar.

Becoming responsible

As he or she becomes incorporated into school life, your child will increasingly take personal responsibility. You're not there to make sure hands are washed before lunch and after going to the lavatory or that coat and boots are neatly put away. Build on this growing independence at home: give him or her more little household tasks to complete, whether it's cleaning shoes or putting out the milk bottles. Establish a morning routine of washing and dressing that your child can eventually manage alone. Personal hygiene is important to health and self-esteem and is largely a matter of habit. While children of five can brush their teeth and hair, wash their faces and dress themselves fairly well, hair-shampooing and running a bath must be supervised. By twelve, at the end of primary school, they should do all of these things and with your encouragement will have learned that the daily routine includes a bath or shower and a clean set of underwear and socks or tights. Many parents get resigned to doing their children's washing and ironing even after they have gone away to college, but there is no reason why an eight-year-old cannot put dirty clothes in the laundry basket, empty the washing machine or help put clothes on the line.

Avoiding infection

Apart from making life pleasanter, personal and domestic hygiene are important in keeping infections at bay. When your child goes to school he or she is likely to catch colds and coughs as well as common childhood ailments like chickenpox which are not serious and which help to build up immunity. Mumps and measles are more serious and can be avoided by immunization at fifteen months.

If you smoke in front of your children you will

irritate the mucous lining of the throat and airways and make them more susceptible to upper respiratory tract infections.

A generally healthy child who is getting enough fresh air, exercise, sleep and food will not get more than a fair share of minor infections. Vitamin supplements may be necessary if the diet is restricted in any way (for a child who refuses milk or will eat neither vegetables or fruit, for example) but remember that it is possible to overdose on vitamins A and D. More is not better. Do not give your child iron supplements without consulting your doctor: they are almost always unnecessary and some types are unsuitable for children.

There are some simple rules to teach schoolchildren which will minimize the risk of spreading infection:
- *never share clothes or food*
- *use paper tissues to blow your nose and flush them down the lavatory*
- *always sneeze into a tissue, if you can*
- *put your hand in front of your mouth when you cough*
- *keep fingernails short and clean*
- *don't pick your nose!*

Immunization against rubella

If your daughter was not given the MMR (Measles, Mumps and Rubella) vaccine at fifteen months, she should be immunized against rubella between the ages of ten and fourteen. Do this whether or not you think she has already had the disease. The symptoms of rubella are minimicked by many other viral infections and she may not have had it, but thought she had. All young girls should be protected by immunization because of the potential threat to an unborn child if they contract the disease when pregnant.

Safety in the home

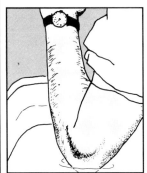

The following guidelines for safety in the home are specifically related to the care of children. There are other important considerations for general safety which fall outside the scope of this list, but also demand our attention.

The newborn baby

• Do not use a pillow in your baby's cot or pram; there is a risk of suffocation. Remove loose protective plastic bags from mattresses; a tight plastic covering moulded to fit cannot lift up and is safe.

Test the temperature of bathwater with your elbow to avoid scalding. It should feel pleasantly warm. Get into the habit of putting cold water in the bath first. If you bathe your baby in the kitchen sink, cover the hot tap with a cloth and make absolutely certain it cannot be turned on accidentally. Never leave a baby alone in the bath. If the phone rings or there is a knock at the door, ignore it, or wrap your baby in a towel and take him or her with you to attend to the caller.

• Do not use lacy shawls in which a baby's fingers could be trapped. Beware of strings on baby bonnets that could tighten round the throat.

• If you leave the pram outside unattended, use a cat net, but remember that this reduces the passage of air and if the pram is in even mild sunlight it can be very hot inside.

• Do not leave a hot water bottle in the baby's bed after warming it. A leak could cause a scald.

• If you smoke, do not light a cigarette or hold one while you are holding your baby. You can easily burn him or her, and anyway the smoke is bad for the child.

• In the car, place your baby in a carry cot secured to the back seat by an approved restraint. Holding your baby on your lap while sitting in the front passenger seat is the most dangerous thing you can do. It is also illegal to have anyone in the front seat who is not wearing a restraint. Putting your own strap around the child is more dangerous than holding a child loose on your lap.

• When buying equipment such as prams, buggies, carry cots and cots, look for a British Standards Institute symbol on the label. This is your guarantee that the product is soundly constructed. Use a shopping tray designed for your pram so that the weight is evenly distributed. Do not hang shopping bags from the handles of a buggy - it could easily tip up and throw the baby out.

• Always use a harness in buggies, baby chairs and baby bouncers.

• Ensure the bars on cots and bannisters are close enough together to prevent a baby's head popping between them.

• When buying a second-hand pram or buggy, take special care to ensure that the brakes on both sides work efficiently and that the rings which prevent it from collapsing are sound. Check that old cots have not been painted with paint containing lead.
• When your baby starts putting things into the mouth, keep out of reach dangerous things such as beads he or she might choke on; a glass with a few drops of alcohol in the bottom; empty plastic pots (like yoghurt pots) that crack easily and have sharp edges.

Six months to one year

• Your baby is still too young to be left alone in the bath.
• During this period you may have to give up using a pram if yours is very lightweight, as your baby will be able to tip it up once able to sit up. Even in a solidly built pram, it is essential to use a harness to prevent the baby falling out.
• Choose a fairly heavy highchair with a wide base. Always use a harness. To save you transferring the harness from pram to highchair at mealtimes, have one for each piece of equipment.
• Once crawling starts, the floor must be cleared of hazards such as dishes of pet food. Any kitchen spills must be mopped up immediately. Central heating radiators and pipes can be very hot to the touch; lower the temperature if necessary. Use a fireguard around open or unit fires. It is against the law to leave a child under twelve years old in a room with an unguarded fire.
• Use plastic covers for electric sockets not in use. Be very careful about flexes trailing across the floor - you may have to dispense with table lamps for a while.
• When your child starts to stand, make sure the furniture is heavy enough to bear his or her weight: tall, thin plant stands, for example, will crash down.
• Instal safety gates at the bottom and top of any flights of stairs now. If there are sets of single steps in a passageway, set an old cushion against them on the lower floor.
• Dispense with tablecloths for the time being - he or she could pull cups of scalding tea on to the head. Clear away

Increasing mobility means you cannot put your baby down in one place and expect him or her to stay there. The child can easily roll off a bed or sofa on to the floor. A playpen is invaluable at this stage, even if you only use it for brief periods.

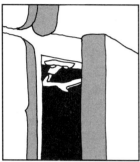

Make your kitchen a safe place now your child is a toddler. Fit all floor cupboards with safety catches so that they cannot be opened, and transfer dangerous substances like cleaning materials and bleach to a high shelf. Fit a cooker guard. Use the back burners on the hob whenever possible. Keep out of reach the flexes of small appliances, such as the kettle, toaster or food processor. Put knives on a magnetic rack on the wall.

glass and china ornaments or put them well out of reach.

The toddler

• It is probably better to do the ironing when your toddler is in bed. A pull on the flex could bring the hot iron down, and the board could trap little fingers. An iron remains dangerously hot for at least half an hour after it has been turned off.

• Keep poisonous substances locked away; not only household chemicals and weedkillers, but drugs (which look like sweets), alcohol and cigarettes. Never let a child play with medicine containers, empty or full. Do not transfer dangerous substances to innocent-looking bottles. Unused medicines should be returned to your pharmacy or flushed down the lavatory. Accidental poisoning is responsible for increasing numbers of child deaths.

• Teach your child to go up and down stairs safely and to use the handrail. Place stops on windows so that they can only be opened a limited amount. Floor-to-ceiling windows can be invisible to a toddler. To prevent him or her crashing into them, let them get dirty or stick transfers on the glass.

• Be careful with toys: make sure they are well made and will not break up into sharp fragments when thrown around (and they will get thrown around). Do not buy objects so small they could be swallowed or pushed into the ears or nostrils.

• A small child can drown in three inches of water: never leave your toddler alone in the bath, and be careful about shallow garden pools: empty them and use them as a sandpit for a few years or cover with protective netting. Go to mother-and-toddler swimming lessons.

• Keep knitting needles, sewing equipment, scissors and DIY equipment in a safe place.

• When walking in a busy street, hold your child's hand firmly or, better still, use a harness and reins if he or she doesn't want to be in the push chair. You can now buy wrist bands connected by a brightly colored flexible cord which give the child a little more independence.

• Have a BSI-approved child seat with harness fitted to the back seat of your car.
• Don't let your toddler play with plastic bags. Dispose of any you don't need safely and quickly and keep the rest where he or she can't get at them.
• You may well not buy any new furniture while your children are still small, but check that none of your existing furniture is made of polyurethane foam. This substance gives off highly toxic fumes when alight and causes suffocation in two to three minutes. Get rid of it, and if you buy second-hand upholstered furniture, make sure it is made of horsehair with a spring construction.
• Store matches out of reach of children.

School-age children should always wear rear seat belts. If you don't have them, get them fitted.

School-age children

As children assume more responsibility around the home, teach them the safety rules you observe yourself. If you let your ten-year-old make a cup of tea or iron the pillowslips, supervise to start with and again from time to time to make sure he or she is being careful.

Safety from strangers

However unlikely it may seem, all children must be protected from the possibility of assault. As they grow, they learn to relate to an ever-wider circle of people. It may see ridiculous to tell a boy or girl not to talk to strangers when you frequently do it yourself: but you can and must tell them not to go with strangers and that you must always know where they are, even if they are going next door to play. If you get separated from your child in a public place, the rule should be for him or her to stay where you were last together, and not to go with anyone who offers to take the child home or anywhere else.

You can explain to older children that while most adults are kind to children, a few are not, and that enticements like sweets or a lift home are danger signals. Discuss the devious ways in which some grown-ups may try to entice a child away, such as saying that they had lost a puppy and would the child come and help the stranger to search. Try to make sure that your child is in a group,

Keep all medication, including contraceptive pills and vitamins, in a lockable cupboard. It should also contain:
- *a thermometer in a safety case*
- *painkillers (analgesics): soluble aspirin and paracetamol for you and junior soluble paracetamol for your child*
- *soothing cream for skin rashes, such as antihistamine*
- *pediatric kaolin and morphine for diarrhea (this has a shelf life of three months).*

A first aid box should contain:
- *adhesive plasters with medicated dressings in assorted sizes*
- *sterile gauze dressings in individual packets*
- *adhesive tape to fix gauze dressings in place*
- *bandages 2.5 and 5 cm (1 and 2 inches) wide*
- *crêpe bandages*
- *tweezers to remove splinters*
- *scissors*
- *cotton wool and paper tissues*
- *safety pins*
- *adhesive tape (to hold cuts together and keep dirt out)*
- *calamine lotion*
- *iodine for washing wounds or an iodine aerosol for spraying on wounds*

because there is some safety in numbers.

By the time a child leaves primary school, he or she should know how to use a public telephone in order to contact you if help is needed. Make sure he or she knows the location of your local police station.

Road safety

It is essential to teach your child road safety and to be seen to observe the rules yourself.

Never let a child under five out alone. He or she can learn that the kerb is the dividing line between pavement and traffic, but easily forgets the danger if attracted by something on the other side of the road, for example. A child is unable to judge the speed of an oncoming vehicle until the age of ten.

When training older children to cross the road, use a basic route and find a spot on the journey which is safe to cross. Insist the child always does so there. Safe places are pedestrian crossings, patrolled crossings, subways or controlled lights, but there may not be any of these on the route to school or the corner shop. Explain the dangers of crossing behind a parked vehicle - the child must make himself or herself visible to drivers. Explain that he or she has to look both ways twice as well as listening for cars, motorbikes and bicycles. Teach your child to judge the speed of traffic (this takes a lot of practice) and to be aware of the unpredictability of drivers, who turn a corner without signalling or signal and keep going straight on. Go over the same route as often as is necessary for you to be sure the child is as safe as you would be yourself. As time goes on, the lessons learned on this basic route can be applied to others, and eventually to all roads.

Minor injuries
Bites

A superficial nip from the family kitten needs no more than washing with soap and hot water. A deep bite from a cat or dog should be cleaned with cotton wool squeezed out in a weak antiseptic solution then sprayed with iodine. Wipe away from the wound, starting at the outer edge and working inwards. Take your child to the doctor. Your child should have been immunized against tetanus in the first year of life, but the doctor will check on this.

Blisters
Whatever the cause of a blister, try not to burst it. Protect it with plaster until it dries out naturally. If it bursts, wash it thoroughly and cover with a dry gauze dressing.

Bruises
While the injury causing a bruise may need treatment, bruises themselves clear up without interference. They occur when blood leaks out of damaged vessels after a blow or fall, and change color because of chemical changes in the blood.

Burns and scalds
Immediately put the affected part, free of clothing, under cold running water and keep it there for ten minutes. Place a clean dressing (not cotton wool) lightly over the skin to prevent infection. Do not use oil, butter or ointment. If the affected area is larger than 2.5 cm (1 inch) take the child to hospital.

Choking
If an object is stuck in the throat, coughing usually dislodges it, but if the airway is blocked this may not be possible. The object must be removed. Hook a finger down your child's throat or turn him or her upside down and thump between the shoulder blades. You can hold a baby or toddler by the feet or turn an older child over your knee.

Cuts and grazes
First clean the injury very thoroughly. Wash your hands before doing this. If any grit or glass is embedded in the cut and you cannot rinse it out with running water, leave

Courses in first aid
The St John Ambulance run first aid courses in many districts, covering practical methods of dealing with accidents and emergencies, including training in mouth-to-mouth resuscitation. It is very wise for at least one adult member of the household to have completed such a course.

it for a doctor to deal with. Use cotton wool squeezed out in a warm antiseptic solution and wipe away from the wound, working from the outer edge inwards. Pat dry with tissues. Spray with iodine. Using tweezers, remove a sterile dressing from its pack, place it over the cut and secure with bandage. If you haven't a dressing big enough to cover the wound, use a freshly-ironed tea towel. Small cuts can be covered with a plaster, or the edges held securely together with Sellotape. Change the dressing often. When the wound is healing well and drying up, leave the dressing off.

Ear damage
If your child gets a foreign body in the ear, do not attempt to remove it. Take him or her to the Accident and Emergency department of your local hospital or your general practitioner.

Eye damage
If a corrosive chemical splashes into the eye, wash it out with plenty of cold water. Lay the child down with the head turned to the side. Hold the eye open and let water run gently downwards over the surface of the eye for at least five minutes. Pat dry, cover with a dry dressing and take the child to hospital or to your general practitioner.

A small piece of grit or an eyelash inside the lower eyelid can be removed by gently pulling down the lid and easing it out with the corner of a handkerchief. If inside the upper lid, pull it down over the lower one and tell your child to look down. This moves the offending object to the corner of the eye and it can easily be removed. If this does not work, and the object is still causing trouble after an hour, take your child to a doctor.

Injuries
Broken bones and suspected internal injuries need urgent medical attention. If your child has a broken ankle, wrist or finger, you can drive him or her to the hospital yourself. A child who is still crying after ten minutes (time this by the clock) and cannot be comforted, has

A-Z of common problems

Allergy

There is a strong inherited tendency in allergy, which can manifest itself in a number of ways, for example breathing difficulties (asthma and hay fever) and skin sensitivity (eczema). Families whose members are allergic are called 'atopic' families. An allergy is a hypersensitivity to proteins (known as allergens), such as house dust mites, pollen, cow's milk or penicillin. The sufferer produces antibodies to these substances which react with them to set off a response. Chemical substances are released which dilate the small blood vessels. Fluid leaks out and causes local swelling. Smooth muscles may go into spasm and mucus secretions pour out. These symptoms can be very distressing, very occasionally life-threatening. Many allergies that begin in childhood lessen in intensity as time goes on, or change in type from a serious complaint like asthma to a milder one like hay fever. Desensitization is a form of treatment given in a series of injections which is useful when the allergen is very difficult to avoid, such as bee and wasp-sting venom, or those which can cause a fatal reaction.

Asthma

Not all specialists agree that

Keep house dust must be kept to a minimum:
- *Don't have dust-trapping objects in the child's room.*
- *Wipe surfaces with a damp cloth rather than a duster.*
- *Use a continental quilt of synthetic fibers rather than blankets.*
- *Mattresses and pillows should be of fire resistant plastic foam or sealed into plastic covers.*
- *Have roller blinds rather than curtains, no cushions or rugs.*

asthma is mainly an allergy, but most treat it as primarily allergic. In an asthma attack mucus is released in the bronchial tubes and the muscles go into spasm. This blocks the airway and makes breathing extremely difficult. The sense of panic attending this terrifying sensation can make matters worse. Besides sensitivity to house dust, asthma attacks can be precipitated by strenuous exercise or emotional stress. *Prevention*: It is essential for parents to join forces with their family doctor in managing asthma. It cannot be cured, but it can be controlled, as far as possible without making the child feel like an invalid. Because an upper respiratory infection can often set off an asthma

attack, do what you can to prevent your child from catching a cold. Increase resistance to infection with vitamin C and keep away from infected persons.

Keeping your child free of emotional stress does not necessarily mean maintaining a falsely calm atmosphere: the child will sense something is wrong anyway. If there is a conflict in the offing, have it out and be done with it: literally, 'clear the air'.

Improved muscle tone and more relaxed breathing are important in keeping attacks at bay. Ask to see a physiotherapist who can advise you about specific exercises as well as ordinary exercise such as swimming which often helps. *Treatment:* Desensitization injections are rarely recommended for asthmatic children. Their effectiveness is debatable and most children find the treatment itself unpleasant.

Drugs are administered both to prevent attacks and to relieve them. They may be given by mouth or inhaled. Modern drugs, correctly used, mean that many children who would once have had to go into hospital can now be treated at home. With the help of a doctor, parents must learn how to give medication in the correct dose and eventually train the child to do so. If your child has an attack that you feel is too serious for you to cope with, get medical help immediately, whatever time it is.

Help your child to lead as normal a life as possible, and remember that the condition usually improves.

Allergic rhinitis (hay fever)

Hay fever is often, but by no means always, associated with asthma. It can occur all year round or only at particular times, depending on the allergen. The most common is pollen, but others are molds and spores (present in the autumn) and house mites in dust. The symptoms are a watery discharge from the nose and swollen nasal passageways giving a blocked feeling. Sometimes the eyes are itchy. Hay fever can occur at any age but generally is not life-long, petering out after a number of years.
Treatment: Avoid the allergen, if known, as far as possible. Keep house dust to a minimum. Consult your doctor about the various drugs available to limit the symptoms. Antihistamines are useful and the modern ones no longer produce drowsiness. If the symptoms are year-round (perennial allergic rhinitis) and severe, desensitization may be recommended.

Bedwetting (enuresis)

Some time during the fourth year most children are able to sleep through the night without urinating, girls achieving this before boys. Some children are slower than others, but if the number of dry nights is slowly increasing, progress is being made. If no progress is evident by age five, or if a child who had achieved dry nights starts to wet the bed again, you may be advised to seek help from your doctor.
Treatment: For 'slow starters', an unhurried and casual approach may well be enough. Talk with your doctor to eliminate any physical causes of bedwetting like worms or urinary infection. Once reassured, relax your own concern, which will certainly communicate itself to your child. Be encouraging and patient, taking all practical measures to reduce the inconvenience of wet bedding. Above all, do not punish your child. Wetting the bed is not his or her fault; ashamed and distressed, the child needs support, not condemnation.

Children who start bedwetting after a long period of being dry are likely to be suffering from anxiety about a particular event. Even when this has been established, 'cure' will not be immediate. Counseling at an enuresis clinic will be helpful and with patience your child will get over the problem.

Bedwetting is much less common in children over seven. At this stage night alarms are sometimes used. These are buzzers which are set off by dampness, and if used in conjunction with counseling their success rate is high.

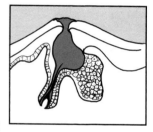

Boils

A boil is an external abscess which forms when the base of a hair follicle (the channel holding the hair root) is infected by a germ. This occurs most frequently where the skin is rubbed by a collar at the neck or pressure on the buttocks. A boil in the ear should be seen by a doctor. Inflammation makes the site painful and red. Within a few days the boil should come to a head and burst to release the pus inside. Do not attempt to burst it yourself, or apply a hot compress because you may spread the infection to adjacent hair follicles. This happens easily even without interference if a child's resistance to infection is impaired for any reason, and a crop of boils ensues. Covering a boil with an antibiotic dressing helps to inhibit the spread of infection. If red streaks appear and nearby glands are painful it means the infection is spreading and you should see a doctor.

Breath-holding
Toddlers who are very bright but easily frustrated may use breath-holding attacks to indicate their intense feelings. This kind of variation on a tantrum is particularly worrying for parents because having turned red, then blue, then grey, their three-year-old may well fall unconscious. At this point he or she will certainly begin to breathe again, and in the intervening few minutes no physical damage will have been done.

Even with this reassurance, most parents would prefer to avoid such attacks, without, however, giving in to their child at the first sign of a tantrum. Keeping conflict to a minimum is easier if you remember that your child is more likely to do what you want if you make the task seem lighthearted rather than precipitate a power struggle between you. Wherever possible, foresee frustrations coming up and steer the child clear with a distraction.

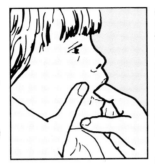

If the child starts to hold the breath, immediately put your index finger into the mouth and hook it round the base of the tongue. Involuntarily the child will take a breath; do this every time it happens and the futility of the exercise will become apparent. Throwing cold water over him or her has no effect at all.

Do not be concerned that your toddler will have an attack in your absence and pass out. Without an audience, preferably including a parent, the drama of breath-holding isn't worth staging.

Chest infections
This general heading embraces infections of the lower respiratory tract - that is: the bronchi, the main air passages from the trachea (windpipe) to the lungs; the bronchioles, small air passages branching out in the lungs; and the alveoli, tiny air sacs at the end of the bronchioles through which

oxygen passes into the bloodstream. Infection in these areas causes similar symptoms though the problems have different sources. A cold or an infected throat can sometimes lead to chest infection, as can some other diseases, such as measles:

Bronchitis
The symptoms of bronchitis are inflammation of the bronchi and extra secretion of mucus within them. A bad cold may develop into bronchitis, attended by wheezy breathing and a thick cough. The temperature may be slightly raised and the child will feel generally unwell.
Treatment: Keep the child warm and rested and give plenty of hot drinks. If necessary your doctor will prescribe analgesics. The most important thing is to clear the air passages of mucus and phlegm by coughing it up so that it can be spat out. Children may swallow the phlegm and vomit it out. Ask your doctor to show you how to 'tip and thump' your child to help bring up phlegm. With care your child will recover within two weeks.

Bronchiolitis
Inflammation of the bronchioles affects babies under eighteen months. Early

symptoms are a cough which quickly develops into rapid, difficult breathing, pale skin tone and difficulty in feeding. *Treatment:* Always call a doctor. If the symptoms are severe, he or she may recommend hospital care so that your baby can have oxygen to help breathing. Bronchiolitis is relatively uncommon but sometimes occurs when the adult population is afflicted with 'flu.

Pneumonia
Acute inflammation of the alveoli may affect only a portion of one lung (lobar pneumonia), or both lungs (broncho-pneumonia). Lobar pneumonia affects older children who are perfectly healthy one day and ill and feverish the next. Broncho-pneumonia affects children under five who already have another infection, not necessarily of the respiratory system, and may not cause a rise in temperature. Your doctor may be able to tell by listening to the chest which part of the lung is affected, or alternatively arrange for an X-ray to be done. The distinctive symptoms of pneumonia are extremely rapid, noisy breathing with flared nostrils. Vomiting may occur and there may be chest pain.
Treatment: Pneumonia is

treated according to the age of your child and the severity of the illness. Occasionally a child will be admitted to hospital for oxygen treatment. Many will be given a course of antibiotics, often after a sample of sputum has revealed the nature of the infecting organism.

Physiotherapy to clear the chest - 'tipping and thumping' - is of great importance. Children whose appetites are depressed should be given high-calorie drinks little and often: lemon and honey, for example, or home-made chicken soup. Recovery is swift but your doctor will want to make a follow-up check to eliminate possible complications.

Chickenpox
Chickenpox is an infection by the same virus that causes shingles (*herpes zoster*) in later life. It is highly infectious, though generally mild, and most common in children under ten. A single occurrence of the disease usually gives immunity. The first sign is a crop of spots,

usually on the chest then spreading to cover an area that would be covered by a T-shirt and shorts, as well as the face and scalp. Sometimes a headache and/or sore throat precedes the rash. The infection is spread mainly by droplets from and to nose and throat. The incubation period is about fourteen days. The spots are flat and pink to begin with, then fill with fluid, thicken and dry out. They are very itchy, but should not be broken as this could lead to secondary infection such as boils. Tiny scars are often left which never disappear.
Treatment: The only treatment necessary is to soothe the itching rash. Dab on calamine lotion whenever necessary. Give baths of warm water with bicarbonate of soda added. Cut the child's nails to prevent them breaking the blisters. As soon as no more new spots appear, the rash gradually declines. If, as rarely happens, your child is badly afflicted with a heavy rash or has chest symptoms, ask your doctor for advice.

Cleft palate
During pregnancy, the roof of the baby's mouth forms in two parts. If they fail to join for any reason the resulting deformity will make it very difficult for your baby to feed without choking.
Treatment: Surgery to repair a

cleft palate is progressive: in the first few days of life, a plate is fitted to the roof of the mouth to facilitate feeding. As the baby grows, this is replaced to fit, until at about eighteen months a final operation is carried out to join the two parts of the natural palate. The success rate for this operation is very high.

Sometimes a cleft palate is accompanied by a harelip, which parents find upsetting because it affects their child's appearance, though it is far less serious. An operation to join the two parts of the lip is carried out at about three months.

Colds

There are hundreds of different viruses responsible for colds, causing infection of the nasal passages. In adult life, and with children of school age, it is impossible to avoid them. With very small babies, however, whose immunity is underdeveloped, a cold can mean such misery that it is sensible to protect them from infection as far as possible. Certainly keep them away from anyone else infected with a cold. The characteristic and familiar symptoms of a cold are a runny nose and cough, watery eyes and a mild sore throat.
Treatment: Ask your doctor for advice if a small baby has a cold which makes breathing

and feeding difficult. The doctor will want to check that there is no other infection causing these symptoms. Nose drops to be used strictly as instructed may be prescribed to clear the air passages before feeding. Nasal aspirators can be used to gently suck the mucus out of the baby's nostrils. Place a small pillow under the mattress at the head end to help breathing.

Older children may need a day in bed or just snuggled up warm on the sofa, but generally can lead a normal life, even playing outside unless it's wet and cold. A stuffy nose can be eased by steam, either a hot drink or sitting in the bath. Your child may lose his or her appetite temporarily but it doesn't matter if you keep the fluid intake up. No medicines are required - indeed, none are effective, with the exception of junior paracetamol for a headache. Syrups which suppress a cough do more harm than good. A cough is a natural reaction to mucus in the throat and prevents it from descending to the lower respiratory tract.

Most colds are past the worst within four days, although a cough at night might persist longer. If a cold hangs around or if any single symptom worsens, consult your doctor.

Eye problems
Conjunctivitis
This occurs when the lining of the eyelids and over the eyeball becomes inflamed, giving rise to the popular name 'pink eye'. It can occur at the same time as another illness, such as measles, or because of a foreign body in the eye, or because of local infection.
Treatment: Take your child to the doctor. If there is a foreign body in the eye, it can be removed. For the infection an antibiotic lotion or drops can be prescribed. The condition should clear up in a matter of days but is highly infectious and contagious. Children should not share towels or flannels and swimming should be avoided.

Squint (strabismus)
The muscles of a newborn baby's eyes are weak, and the eyes may appear to converge. As the muscles strengthen, by about three months, this rights itself naturally. Any divergence after this time may be a true squint and should be referred to your doctor. To see properly, both eyes must work together to send 'matching' images to the brain. If one eye is incorrectly aligned, the images diverge, and the brain will ignore the incorrect one coming from the bad eye. The term 'lazy eye' should be discouraged as

it belies the seriousness of this condition; for if it continues the 'bad' eye will stop working and go blind. Squints must be diagnosed as early as possible so that they can be treated. There is a strong family tendency to squints.

Treatment: In order to strengthen the misaligned eye, your child's good eye can be covered with a patch, or the child can be given

spectacles with one side blanked out. When old enough he or she can be taught exercises to improve the muscles controlling eye movement. If the muscles themselves are unequal, surgery may be recommended to correct the difference. Squints should be treated before the age of four if permanent damage is to be avoided.

Styes

A stye is an infection in the hair follicle of an eyelash, causing pain and swelling which eventually comes to a head and discharges the pus within.

Treatment: Apply heat to the stye. Cover the bowl end of a wooden spoon with lint or a bandage and dip it in very hot salt water. Apply this compress to the eye, holding it in place for ten minutes. Repeat every three hours. If the stye does not come to a head after three days or if your child suffers from a series of styes, consult your doctor. To prevent styes, make sure everyone uses their own facecloth and towel.

Eczema

Eczema rarely appears before two to three months of age and often disappears by the end of the third year, though it may flare up again in later life at times of stress. The first sign is usually a bright red, scaly patch on the cheek which is very itchy. It also appears in the groin, the forearm and behind the knee, and can be more widespread. No single cause has been identified, but a sensitivity to cow's milk does seem to be a factor. Breastfeeding is best, and after weaning use soya milk rather than cow's milk until the phase has passed. Like asthma, eczema is aggravated by emotional disturbance. An asthmatic child may have eczema, or vice versa, but the advent of the one often means the

abating of the other.

Treatment: Like asthma, eczema has no cure. Control is by means of ointments to soothe the inflamed skin. Cortisone creams are very effective if applied thickly as instructed by your doctor but long-term use thins and damages the skin. Tar-based ointments are messy but can be used liberally. The irritation is so intense that it will be very difficult to stop your child scratching and breaking the skin. Keep the fingernails short and give the child a jar of tar ointment to smear on instead of scratching. The skin must be kept clean. Soap and water is too drying. Use olive oil or mineral oil on cotton wool to gently wipe it clean, or use liquid paraffin before applying tar ointment.

Putting your child into heavy woollen clothes will make the itching unbearable. Use soft, silky, loose clothing wherever possible. Stopping the scratching is important, but it isn't easy. Providing some distraction works best; a sedative may be prescribed to help your child sleep at night.

Foot and leg problems
Bow legs

Up to the age of two, your child will naturally have slightly bow legs, which will straighten out without interference. Wearing a very bulky nappy will emphasize the outward curve of the legs and may inhibit their becoming straight. Use neat disposables during the day. A tendency for bow legs runs in families. Bow legs caused by rickets are a rarity now that children have enough vitamin D but are occasionally seen in Asian children living in this country because their skins are unable to manufacture sufficient amounts of the vitamin under the weaker English sun.

Flat feet
The feet and legs of a baby who is just learning to walk look rather different from those of an active five-year-old. The feet appear flat because they are fat, and as the child becomes slimmer, the problem resolves. If your school-age child seems to have slightly flat feet, get him or her to stand on tiptoe and you will see the arch form. Standing on tiptoe and walking are the best exercises to improve foot shape.

Ingrown toenails
When the outer edge of the toenail presses into the flesh it can be very painful. No home treatment is effective - ask your doctor to refer you to a chiropodist. Proper care of the feet will prevent this condition. Always cut the toenail into a square shape; never clean the sides of the nails by digging with a sharp instrument, and make sure there is plenty of toe-room in your child's shoes.

In-toeing
A child who has just started walking finds it easier to stay balanced by turning the toes in slightly. As confidence increase, walking gets straighter. If you think your child looks uncomfortable walking, check that socks and shoes are not too tight.

Knock knees
Between the ages of three and seven a tendency to knock knees is common, and is more likely in an overweight child. Again, no treatment is necessary as the condition rights itself as the child grows and gets thinner.

'Flu
See *Influenza*

Gastroenteritis
Gastroenteritis means inflammation of the gastro-intestinal tract - the stomach lining and the intestines. The term is used to describe the symptoms of diarrhea caused by some kind of infection, whether or not accompanied by fever and vomiting. For treatment, see diarrhea. Occurrences in babies are generally caused by bacteria in milk that has been unhygienically prepared or has been left to stand. In older children and adults there are any number of organisms that might be

To prevent germs breeding in food, it is essential to observe strict hygiene in the preparation of meals and to cook and serve them properly.
• *Wash your hands before preparing food and make your family wash theirs before eating it.*
• *Boiling and pasteurizing destroy bacteria in ten minutes but destroys vitamin C.*
• *All cooked food is best eaten directly after cooking.*
• *Bacteria breed best at room or body temperature - never keep cooked meat, fish, egg and milk dishes in warm surroundings more than one or two hours.*
• *In the cold germs breed slowly. In the refrigerator germs live but do not breed. Make sure your refrigerator is cold enough.*
• *Be doubly careful when using a microwave oven that food is cooked evenly and completely. If your oven is a low wattage, ready-prepared meals may take longer to cook than stated by the manufacturer.*

responsible, and in most cases investigation is not worthwhile. Severe gastro-enteritis can be caused by food poisoning.

Glandular fever *(infectious mononucleosis)*
Glandular fever rarely causes classic symptoms and often passes undiagnosed. It is caused by a virus which is transmitted by close contact, particularly kissing an infected person, but you don't always get the disease just because you are exposed to the virus. The first sign is a severe sore throat accompanied by a feeling of lethargy, loss of appetite and a feverish headache. The glands in the neck, armpit and groin are swollen. The spleen may be enlarged enough to be detected by a doctor. Symptoms persist for up to three weeks in adults, a shorter time in children, but it can take up to eight weeks for the patient to feel completely better. A feeling of lethargy after the illness can be very long lasting.
Treatment: A blood test will confirm the diagnosis but most pediatricians prefer not to do this. While the symptoms persist, bed rest in an airy room with plenty to drink and analgesics if needed is the best treatment. Give your child plenty of time to recover, and let him or her

take things easy for a month or so after contracting the illness. Sport and rough games may damage the enlarged spleen.

Hernia
Some new babies develop small swellings near the umbilicus (umbilical hernias), because the muscles of the abdominal wall are not yet strong enough to prevent the stomach bulging out, especially when the baby cries. At one time babies with umbilical hernias were strapped up but this is not now thought necessary as hernias usually disappear without treatment in the first year, and the majority have gone by the age of five.

A hernia in the groin (an inguinal hernia) is less common, but sometimes affects baby boys in their first year especially if they have an undescended testicle. It appears as a swelling in the

groin, where a loop of intestine bulges through an opening in the abdominal muscle wall. When your baby is lying down, the loop should slip back in and the swelling disappears.
Treatment: Consult your doctor, who will arrange for a simple operation to repair the opening in the abdominal wall. If the hernia does not disappear when your baby is lying down the operation may have to be done promptly as the bulging loop of intestine will be deprived of its blood supply.

Influenza
Influenza is caused through infection by a virus, transmitted by droplets from nose and throat. There are any number of different strains, with new ones appearing all the time. Mercifully, it is a less severe illness in childhood, though the symptoms are similar to those suffered by an adult: sore throat, blocked nose and feverish headache at the start, quickly followed by aching limbs and shivering. This lasts at most four days, with two or three days' convalescence. Influenza leaves a feeling of general depression that can take rather longer to throw off.
Treatment: Antibiotics do not kill viruses, but if your child has a secondary infection, in

the throat, for example, they may be prescribed.

Laryngitis

Laryngitis is an inflammation of the larynx (voice-box), usually occurring at the same time as the cold whose virus caused it, or as a result of another infection of the upper respiratory tract. Symptoms are hoarseness or temporary loss of voice, an irritating cough, sore throat and slight fever.

Treatment: Encourage your child to rest the voice. Keep the temperature down with paracetamol along with plenty to drink. If you smoke, do not do so in your child's presence. Recovery should follow two or three days' rest, but if the condition does not improve within a week, consult your doctor.

Lice

There are a number of lice which infest the human body, but children are particularly prone to headlice, small, flat wingless insects which are brownish-grey in color. They live by sucking blood from the scalp and lay eggs which they attach to the base of the hair. They spread from child to child by direct contact and also from things such as combs, towels and hats. Symptoms include acute itching and small, oval shiny yellow eggs on the hairs

which are difficult to remove. You can confirm the diagnosis by brushing the child's hair forward over a sheet of white paper. Dislodged lice will show up clearly against the white.

Treatment: Treat with lotion recommended by the pharmacist. Regular hair brushing damages the adult lice and prevents them from laying eggs.

Measles

Measles is one of the most infectious of the childhood illnesses and is caused by a virus which spreads through the air in tiny droplets of moisture. The first signs are like that of a heavy cold. The eyes are sore and inflamed, the nose runny and the cough troublesome. The temperature is high. Diagnosis may be made at this stage by the presence of Koplik's spots which look like grains of salt on the insides of the cheeks just above the lower teeth at the back of the mouth. Sometimes the child seems

much better for twenty-four hours, only to worsen again. The rash begins two to four days after the cold symptoms, starting behind the ears and spreading to the face before appearing on the trunk. As the rash spreads, the fever abates.

The usual complication following measles is getting another infection on top of it. This is generally caused by a bacterium which invades either the ear or the lungs. If the child deteriorates on the fourth day of the rash, then suspect something else has happened. Youngsters under two years are particularly at risk from this type of secondary infection, so if the fever does not abate, or after the third day of the rash the cough worsens, or the child has earache, call the doctor. Antibiotics have no effect on viruses, so cannot be used to combat the measles germ itself. However, your doctor may prescribe antibiotics to clear up a secondary infection. There are some other very rare complications; inflammation of the brain (meningitis) is one (it occurs once in every million cases). However, remember that ear problems are by far the most likely.

Treatment: There isn't any except to make your child feel as comfortable as possible with warm drinks, paracetamol to reduce fever, aches and pains, and lots of tender loving care.

There is now an effective vaccine which can safely be given to most children. Measles is a very unpleasant illness. It can be prevented. Complications following the vaccine are ten times rarer than those following the natural disease. Measles is so infectious that almost all children will catch it if they have not been vaccinated.

Mumps

Mumps is a moderately infectious disease which rarely affects children under five. It is transmitted by droplets to and from nose and throat. The virus passes into the bloodstream and may affect other parts of the body.

The incubation period is about twenty-one days. In childhood most instances are mild, twenty-five per cent of children have mumps and recover without anyone realizing it. Children are most unlikely to get mumps again, as one instance gives immunity.

The virus affects the parotid glands which lie in front of the ear. These are salivary glands, and one symptom is dryness in the mouth. One or other gland swells up, sometimes both, and the pain makes it difficult to eat. Occasionally your child may have a fever and feel slightly unwell.

Inflammation of the testicles in boys who have reached puberty and in adults, is a rare complication, but one that causes a great deal of concern. The effects of such inflammation may result in temporary sterility, but the sperm count picks up rapidly. Such problems can be eliminated if your child has the MMR vaccine (page 49).

Treatment: Call your doctor to confirm the diagnosis. He or she will recommend an analgesic if your child is in much pain. A soft scarf wrapped around the neck is comforting. Lots of nourishing drinks are essential, not only because eating is difficult but to relieve dryness in the mouth. In the absence of saliva, which is antiseptic, there is a risk of mouth infection: get your child to rinse out the mouth regularly and keep the teeth clean. The swelling should subside within a week. If other glands are tender or painful, consult your doctor.

Nappy rash

The delicate skin of a newborn baby is sensitive to the urine and feces contained in a wet or soiled nappy. The skin looks bright pink and blotchy, and is obviously sore. Thrush (see page 70), a fungus which normally lives in the intestines, may complicate nappy rash, but ammonia dermatitis is the most common kind: ammonia is produced by a chemical reaction between urine and feces, and has a distinctively acrid smell. Infected nappy rash caused by incompletely sterilized nappies produces yellow spots and sores.

Treatment: Prevention is better than cure - though even the best-cared-for babies have nappy rash at some time or another. Breastfed babies are less likely to have nappy rash because breast milk is not as alkaline as cow's milk. Change your baby's nappy as often as you can, and certainly as soon as it is soiled. Use a one-way nappy liner which lets urine through to the nappy but not back again, and helps to keep your baby's bottom dry. Leave off plastic pants occasionally; better still, let your baby lie on a nappy with a naked bottom whenever possible. Be scrupulous about sterilizing nappies, if you use the terry-towelling kind (see page 36 and 37) and do not use enzyme washing powders or unnecessary fabric softeners. Nappies that blow dry in the fresh air or in a tumble drier are softer than those dried over heat indoors and less irritating to the skin: friction increases the rash. Apply a protective barrier cream or castor oil cream after cleaning your baby and before putting on a fresh nappy. If the rash becomes infected, see your doctor. With good management and hygiene this should not happen. As your baby gets older and the skin toughens up, the incidence of nappy rash should diminish, though the need to prevent it still prevails.

Nail-biting
A great many children of school age bite their nails at some time, whether because they're bored or nervous or because the habit is soothing. It is probably best not to draw attention to it unless the habit becomes compulsive, the nails are always bitten down to the quick and the child is obviously anxious. Treat the cause, not the symptom, by smoothing out whatever is worrying the child and helping him or her to become relaxed. Punishments will only exacerbate the situation. With older children, moderate nail-biting can sometimes be phased out with tactful references to how much nicer well-manicured hands look.

Night terrors
After about age four, children are more likely to have vivid dreams and nightmares. Night terrors, as they are called, are of a different order: they usually occur in the first two hours of sleep; the child wakes up suddenly, screaming with fear. He or she is not fully conscious and may not even recognize you. These emotional disturbances are probably connected to some experience in the child's life - perhaps a stay in hospital that involved an unpleasant examination, or seeing a cat run over by a car - which aroused deep unspoken fears.
Treatment: You will obviously rush to your child the minute he or she screams, but do not try to shake the child fully awake. Keep him or her in bed, held in a secure embrace, and the child will probably go back to sleep in a few minutes. While a bad dream can be explained and defused in conversation the next day, night terrors cannot be rationalized away. As your child's confidence and sense of security grows, the attacks will pass. If they persist or grow more frequent, talk to your doctor about the problem.

Pertussis *(whooping cough)*
Whooping cough is an extremely serious infectious disease and can be fatal to babies under one year old. It is caused by a bacterium. No immunity is passed on from mother to baby so immunization is given at three, five and nine months unless contraindicated. Immunized children may still contract the disease but it will be much less severe. The infection spreads by coughing and invades the air passages of the lungs, which can be permanently damaged. The incubation period is about fourteen days.

The first symptoms are a runny nose, slightly raised temperature and a cough. The cough gets steadily worse until it occurs in frightening spasms many times a day, often causing the child to vomit. 'Whooping' is the sound made as the child fights to inhale, but babies often do not whoop. The younger the child, the greater the risk of dehydration, exhaustion and weight loss.
Treatment: Call your doctor. If a diagnosis of whooping

cough is made in the early stages a course of antibiotics may limit its severity. Sedatives may be prescribed to help your child rest at night. Cough medicines are of no use. Stay with your child to provide reassurance during a fit of coughing; hold a baby upright during an attack. Give small amounts of nourishing food and drink as often as possible. Depending on severity, the acute stage of the illness may last three weeks, with a troublesome cough persisting for months.

Ringworm

Ringworm occurs on the skin (*tinea corporis*), the feet (*tinea pedis*) and the scalp (*tinea capitis*). It is a fungus infection that can be picked up from animals or from another person. Each member of the family should have his or her own facecloth and

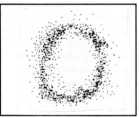

towel. Never share hairbrushes or combs.
Tinea corporis (above) produces circular rashes that grow from the size of a pimple larger and larger while

healing at the center. They may be itchy. The outer edge of the ring is the active area of the infection.
Treatment: your doctor will prescribe an anti-fungal cream and the rash should fade and heal in a few weeks.
Tinea capitis is most common in children. The scalp may be itching, then patches of inflammation appear, from where the hair breaks off, leaving almost bare patches.
Treatment: The doctor will take a scraping from the inflamed area to identify the fungus before prescribing an appropriate shampoo

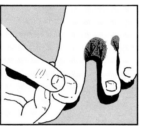

treatment. It may take one or two months to clear.
Tinea pedis (athlete's foot, above) occurs on the sole of the foot and between the toes. It is more common in older children who go to public swimming pools, for example. The skin becomes red, cracked and itchy.
Treatment: Keep the feet perfectly dry and use an anti-fungal cream or powder. Change socks daily.

All forms of ringworm call for high standards of personal hygiene to prevent the infection spreading from one part of the body to another and from person to person. Change your child's clothes daily, laundering the dirty clothes as soon as possible.

Roseola infantum

This moderately infectious disease affects children under three. It is caused by a virusand spread by droplets from nose and throat to nose and throat. It is mild in effect and may pass undiagnosed. Often the first symptom is a high fever, up to 105°F/ 40.5°C, which will make your child feel very unwell. This stage lasts several days. After the fever abates, a rash of small pink spots appears on the back and chest, and may spread further. The rash disappears rapidly.
Complications: With a high fever there is a risk of convulsions, so keep your child cool by sponging with tepid water and using only a cotton sheet as a cover. Give plenty to drink.
Treatment: Call your doctor. Before the characteristic rash appears a diagnosis may be difficult but the doctor may prescribe medication to reduce the fever. Your child will want to rest anyway while the temperature is high.

Rubella *(German measles)*
German measles, which is nothing to do with ordinary measles, is a mild virus infection spread by droplets to and from nose and throat. The incubation period is fourteen to twenty-one days. An affected child may have a sore throat, followed within two days by a rash that starts behind the ears and on the forehead before spreading over the body. Sometimes it simply looks as if the child is flushed. The glands at the back of the neck may be enlarged. Because diagnosis is difficult rubella often goes undetected. No special treatment is necessary.

Immunization against rubella is essential, not because it is a dangerous illness in itself but because of the immense danger it poses for an unborn child. The baby of a pregnant woman who contracts rubella in the first three months of her pregnancy can suffer from deafness, blindness and severe heart defects. All children should be immunized to protect the community at large, and in the case of girls to protect their unborn children. If your children do get rubella, keep them isolated at home for seven days.

Scarlet fever
Scarlet fever can affect children of any age. Nowadays this disease is rare but the complications are very serious. It is a streptococcal throat infection with a rash, and the first symptoms resemble those of tonsillitis: a sore throat, fever, inflamed tonsils, headache and vomiting. Within twenty-four hours a rash made up of innumerable tiny red spots appears on the neck and chest, spreading over the entire body. After about a week the skin flakes off the spots.
Treatment: Call your doctor, who will probably prescribe antibiotics to limit the illness and to prevent secondary infection of the kidneys or rheumatic fever, both of which are much more serious than scarlet fever itself. Complete the course of antibiotics. Your child will need rest during the fever but should be better within a week.

Sleeping problems
Many babies and small children have problems getting to sleep or wake frequently in the night; a very few suffer from night terrors when upset (see page 67). Other specific problems are recurrent nightmares and sleepwalking.

Nightmares rarely affect children under the age of four, and usually occur after a particularly strenuous or exciting day. Imaginative children are most likely to have vivid, frightening dreams, especially following a scary film or television programme. Unlike night terrors, a child woken by a nightmare is quickly reassured that 'it was just a dream' and easily soothed back to sleep. Monitor the television viewing of an excitable child and make sure the hour before bedtime is relaxing.

Sleepwalking usually affects children between the ages of ten and fourteen, and often coincides with a period of stress such as taking exams, fading away when the source of the stress is dealt with or passes. It generally takes place within two hours of falling asleep: the child gets out of bed and wanders about wide-eyed, but does not attempt any complex action. The best way of dealing with it is to gently lead him or her back to bed again; it won't do any harm to wake the child, but it won't do any good either, trying to explain how he or she happens to be in the kitchen at midnight in pyjamas. If your child goes through a phase of sleepwalking, it is as well to take practical measures to prevent injury. Close the bedroom windows tight; use a stairgate; lock and bolt the front and back doors at night to stop the child leaving the house before you know what's happening. Sleepwalking is rarely a sign of profound emotional disturbance, but more likely of a temporary anxiety which a perceptive parent can relieve.

Sunburn

Whether or not the adult fashion for a deep tan passes now that its dangers are known, babies and children need particular protection from the sun's rays, as the skin of infants is very delicate. The pain of sunburn becomes evident after the damage is done. Because your child will not complain about it while the damage is actually occuring, you must be aware of the dangers. Use sunblock screening creams on every exposed part of the body, re-applying them frequently and whenever your child has been in the sea or swimming pool. Encourage him or her to wear a hat and to play in the shade.

If you leave your baby outside in the pram on a sunny day, place the pram in the shade and move it as the sun moves.
Treatment: Cool sunburned skin with tepid, not cold, water, in whatever way causes least discomfort, perhaps standing the child in the bath and using a shower-head or pouring water from a bowl. Choose soft, light clothing. Keep the child out of the sun. If blisters form, consult your doctor, as there is a risk of infection and scarring if they are carelessly treated.

Speech therapy

Individual children differ in the pace at which they develop. It is natural for children to go through a period of hesitancy in speech, accompanied by repetition and stammering, reflecting the difference in speed between what they're thinking and their ability to say it. This settles down in time, as long as you listen patiently and ignore 'mistakes'.

It is probably worth consulting the child health clinic staff about a child's speech, if: at eighteen months he or she has made no attempt to use words; at two, cannot put two words together; and is not able to speak intelligibly at the age of three.

Hearing properly is vital to

proper speech development: very few children are irretrievably deaf, and those few will have speech therapy, but the first line of treatment is always aimed at improving the hearing. Repeated ear infections are likely to slow down speech development. If your child has a speech defect such as a lisp or, for example, still says 'tat' instead of 'cat' at the age of six to seven, you should consult your doctor about correcting it before the fault becomes a fixed habit. Good clear speech is crucial to effective communication. Unintelligible or halting speech can be a tremendous drawback to the development of a confident, outgoing personality. Speech therapy to improve fluency can be given at special clinics, in hospitals or in schools. Much of the work is in the form of games, and it is very important that supportive, follow-up work is done at home. Beware of quick 'quack' cures: they are useless and can be harmful. Effective speech therapy requires patience and should be conducted by trained professionals.

Thrush

Thrush is caused by a fungus infection called *Candida albicans.* It occurs in adults when resistance to infection is lowered and in newborn

babies because such resistance has not been built up. The most frequent site of infection in babies is the mouth, which gets covered with white patches that look like milk curds. These cannot be wiped away and they make feeding difficult. Because the fungus is present in the stools, it can also affect the nappy area, causing a particular kind of rash.
Treatment: For thrush in the mouth your doctor may recommend the traditional remedy of gentian violet paint, but this is messy. The most commonly prescribed medication now is an antibiotic called nystatin in liquid form to be applied by dropper. It is available as a cream for the buttocks. The infection may take two weeks to clear.

Thumb-sucking
Babies suck their thumbs not only because it gives them comfort and pleasure but because it is part of exploration and learning. There is no reason to discourage it. Many babies give it up anyway by the end of the second year. Those who do not are not especially insecure or retarded: it is for them an aid to relaxation like a cuddly toy or comfort blanket. You need only be concerned if an older child sucks the thumb for long

periods instead of playing and seems otherwise anxious. It is important to find the source of the trouble and put it right. Thumb-sucking does not damage the set of the teeth unless it continues beyond age six and is for prolonged periods.

Tonsillitis
The tonsils are at the back of the throat. Like the adenoids, they are composed of lymphoid tissue which traps harmful organisms from entering the body. Tonsillitis is the term used to describe inflammation of the tonsils, which may have various causes. A sore throat may or may not be an accompanying symptom, but the tonsils will be bright red and your child will probably have a fever, headache, feel generally unwell and have a bout of vomiting. The child may complain of referred pain in the ear.
Complications: A middle-ear infection may develop. If the bacterium streptococcus has caused the inflammation, kidney inflammation or rheumatic fever may ensue.
Treatment: Call your doctor. If the cause is a bacterial infection he or she will prescribe antibiotics to prevent complications. Give your child plenty to drink as solid food may be difficult to manage.

Let your child stay in bed for a day or two if desired. He or she should feel better within a week. Tonsillitis is infectious, so it is best to keep other children away until recovery is complete.

Tummy ache
When babies cry, whatever the cause, they draw up their legs - this alone is no indicator of abdominal pain. If your baby cannot be comforted, however, and is off feeds, he or she is probably in pain. Call your doctor, particularly if your baby is pale, vomiting and suffering from diarrhea which seems to be accompanied by pain. Blood in the stools may indicate an obstruction in the bowel: this is serious and needs urgent attention. Children often use 'tummy ache' to describe a pain somewhere else or when they feel sick. Don't ignore a child's complaint about pain: ask where it hurts and if in any doubt call your doctor. Tonsillitis, for example, can cause abdominal pain and may need special treatment. Recurrent abdominal pain very often has an emotional cause. The source of the stress may be worry about school, especially among children who have, or who have been given, very high standards to meet. Another frequent source of worry is

food, in a family where 'clearing your plate' is the rule or where undue attention is paid to the working of a child's bowels. Ask your doctor or health visitor to help you uncover the source of the trouble, and find ways to help your child relax, while reassuring him or her that, although you know that your child is in real discomfort, there is nothing dangerously wrong.

Urinary infections
It is more difficult to diagnose urinary infections in babies and children than it is in adults. The symptoms that might present themselves, (loss of appetite, a rise in temperature, vomiting) can have numerous causes. You probably won't notice if a baby in nappies is urinating more frequently than usual; but in an older child this may be more obvious, and he or she may tell you if it hurts or if there is blood in the urine. *Treatment:* Take your child to your doctor. To diagnose an infection of the bladder or kidneys a specimen of urine will be needed. Treatment will be with antibiotics, and although the infection clears up quickly, your doctor will want to check urine specimens for some time to make sure it does not flare up again.

Verrucas
Verrucas are warts on the feet. Like all warts, they are caused by a virus, and may appear in groups. Because verrucas are infectious a child (or adult) who has them should not walk barefoot until they have disappeared. *Treatment:* Most warts clear up without treatment, though they may last for as long as eighteen months. Because verrucas can make walking painful, you can ask your doctor for specific treatment. He or she may prescribe an ointment, have the wart cut out or freeze it off.

Vomiting
Many new babies regurgitate a spoonful or two of milk after a feed. This is called 'possetting', is normal, and causes the baby no distress. A frequent cause of true vomiting is taking in too much air with a feed: check the size of the teat on his or her bottle or check with your health visitor that your breastfeeding position is correct. Recurrent vomiting accompanied by diarrhea and loss of appetite is a symptom of illness and should be referred to your doctor promptly.

If a child vomits once, appears quite well afterwards and you can identify the cause as overeating at a birthday party, for example, there is no cause for alarm. If there are

any other symptoms - headache, diarrhea, fever, loss of appetite, abdominal pain - your child is ill and you should call your doctor.

Worms
Some worms are parasites that live in the intestine. They affect twenty per cent of children from every background, whether their homes are spotless or not. The most common type are nematode threadworms, which can be seen as tiny white threads moving in the stools and around the anus. They cause local irritation when they come out to lay their eggs. This is worst at night. Girls may also suffer from severe itching around the vulva. A child scratches, puts the thumb back in the mouth and the cycle starts again. *Treatment:* Worms are easily eliminated with special medicine, either in a single dose or a short course. Each member of the family should be treated. Keep your child's fingernails very short and clean to prevent the eggs being trapped there.

Less avoidable problems

The child in hospital

Babies and small children are deeply dependent on their parents. For them to be separated is distressing enough; to endure a strange environment, strange faces, and possibly unpleasant medical procedures is no less than terrifying. It follows that if a child goes into hospital, if at all possible one parent should be there all the time. In practical terms the ease with which you can meet this need differs from hospital to hospital. Many, but not all, have wards specially adapted for parents and children. In others all-day visiting is standard. If you are to spend several days in hospital with your child, make sure you both get plenty of visitors; if your child spends long stretches of time asleep, you may even be able to help with some of the other children.

Sharing the care of your child with the hospital staff needs a little diplomacy: help them and your child by encouraging him or her to do what must be done to get well, taking medicine when necessary or having an injection.

If your child is admitted as an emergency, he or she may not at first be seen by staff familiar with the special needs of young patients, and your supportive presence will be even more important. Certain procedures may need your specific assistance, such as having stitches. Help to keep your child still - talk gently, get him or her to talk to you as a distraction from what's happening. When a blood sample is being taken from a vein in the arm, it's probably best to position the child so that he or she cannot see.

In hospital as in normal life, children's play is a vital part of well-being. Many children's wards have a member of staff called a play specialist, trained to understand how children express their feelings in play and to help them through what can be a difficult experience. This kind of therapy undoubtedly speeds recovery, and certainly makes a child's time in hospital more pleasant. Like all the staff on a children's ward, the play specialist should be happy to talk to you about your child's health and progress.

Prepare your child for going into hospital by explaining why it is necessary (to make a tummy stop hurting, for example.) There is a risk that he or she will see the experience as a punishment if you don't. Don't be vague about which part of the body is to be operated on - children have some idea of anatomy, and a simple drawing might help. Alternatively, use a doll as a model. Explain that you will be near all through the operation and immediately afterwards, and warn your child of any pain or discomfort there might be. If you have time to plan for a stay in hospital, you can find out how the children's ward is run so that he or she knows what to expect. Don't forget to pack a favorite toy or comfort blanket and let the staff know that he or she needs it.

Inherited disorders are carried by abnormal genes by one or both parents. A parent with a dominant abnormal gene will himself or herself suffer from the disorder, and although the other partner is normal, one in two of their children are likely to be carriers, the chances of them having an affected child is 50:50. A parent with a recessive abnormal gene will not have the disorder. If his or her partner is normal, the chances are that one in two of their children will suffer from it; two in four will be carriers, but unaffected, and one in four will neither carry it nor be affected.

When your child goes home, give him or her time to settle back into the usual routine. A toddler may take a temporary backward step in toilet training; sleep patterns may be disturbed for a while. This is natural after a major disturbance in a child's life, but love and patience wins through in the end.

Congenital abnormalities

A congenital disorder is one that is present though not necessarily evident, at birth. It may or may not be inherited. Parents who have had a child with such a disorder, or have anyone in their families with an inherited disorder, are advised to seek genetic counseling. This can be arranged through your doctor. The aim of genetic counseling is to give parents correct information about the likelihood of their having subsequent children who might be affected with the disorder in question, and how likely it is that their children will in their turn give birth to affected babies. Genetic counselors give informed and sympathetic advice; they do not lay down rules. The most commonly encountered inherited conditions are discussed below.

Hemoglobinopathies

There are a number of blood disorders passed on by inheritance. They include sickle cell anemia, which is particularly common among people of Afro-Caribbean origin, and thalassemia, usually affecting people of Mediterranean origin but also known in Arab people and those from the Indian sub-continent. Blood tests to detect these disorders should be done at the first ante-natal check-up if there is any likelihood of their incidence, but such tests can be done before pregnancy if you wish. Both disorders are serious types of anemia. In both cases, the baby's skin and the whites of the eyes are slightly yellow in color (jaundice). Throughout childhood the sufferer will be prone to feverishness and weakness; sickle cell anemia can give rise to blood clots in any part of the body, and strenuous exercise will result in deep, rapid breathing. Both conditions are chronic and endure through life.

Complications of sickle cell anemia are ulcers, priapism (permanent erection) and infections of the bones, kidneys and other organs, which may be life-threatening. There is no cure for thalassemia or sickle cell anemia at present. Treatment is by blood transfusion, which must be performed regularly in order to sustain life.

Phenylketonuria (PKU)

PKU is a biochemical disorder affecting mental development. The parents of babies with PKU have no symptoms themselves, but each of them carries the relevant recessive gene, and the affected child has two recessive genes. Not all their children will be so affected.

Within the first few days of life, all babies are tested for PKU (a pinprick of blood is taken from the heel of the foot). Untreated, PKU leads to mental handicap; but if the baby is put on a special diet at an early stage, he or she will develop quite normally. Research is being carried out to find out whether the diet needs to be observed for life (see right-hand column).

Deafness

Some cases of deafness are inherited. Other causes are German measles in the first thirteen weeks of pregnancy: taking certain drugs in pregnancy; syphilis in the mother, and brain damage at birth. Both ears or one only may be affected and the hearing loss may not be total. The first signs are a lack of response to sounds, particularly the mother's voice when she is out of sight, and later, poor speech development or none.

Color blindness

The inability to distinguish colors is an inherited defect affecting many more boys than girls. Usually the difficulty lies in telling the difference between red and green; total color blindness covers the spectrum.

This defect causes no special problems. Some

Hearing tests
These are a prominent feature of all developmental checks held at your Child Health Clinic, but if you suspect that your child's hearing may be impaired, ask for more detailed tests to be carried out. The earlier deafness, to whatever degree, is diagnosed, the better able you are to ensure that your child's cognitive and social development is not held up. A hearing aid may be fitted if suitable. Many deaf children attend normal schools and do well, with an understanding teacher. Children with total hearing loss attend special schools to help them cope with their disability. A deaf child is as intelligent as one that can hear, but has to try harder and needs special attention to fulfil his or her full potential.

companies ask prospective employees to do a color test where safety at work might be affected.

Pyloric stenosis

Pyloric stenosis runs in families, first-born baby boys being affected four times as often as girls. The pylorus is an area of the stomach which opens into the small intestine. In babies predisposed to the disease, feeding causes muscle in the wall of the stomach to thicken and obstruct the outlet. As a result, within two to six weeks of birth, the baby starts to vomit after feeds. Unlike the dribble of possetting, the vomit is projectile, shooting out as if from a spout. The baby becomes hungry, constipated and fails to gain weight. If not promptly treated, there is a danger of starvation and dehydration. Your doctor can diagnose pyloric stenosis by gently feeling the pylorus while the baby is feeding (a characteristic of this type of vomiting is that the baby doesn't suffer appetite loss). Treatment is by a simple operation; results are excellent and the digestion is normal afterwards.

Epilepsy

Epilepsy sometimes runs in families. Often the underlying cause is unknown. It may be caused by birth injury or following on from meningitis or encephalitis. The seizures characterizing epilepsy are caused by an abnormal discharge of electrical activity from part of the brain. It is emphatically not a mental illness and does not in any way predispose the sufferer to mental illness. There are two main kinds of fit (see left-hand column). In both cases a doctor will confirm the diagnosis with an electroencephalogram (a test to monitor electrical activity in the brain). Epilepsy can be treated with anti-convulsant drugs which enable the sufferer to lead an almost normal life (in adulthood, driving a car may not be possible and drinking alcohol may interfere with the efficiency of the drugs). Regular monitoring is important as the dosage of the drug may need to be adjusted periodically. Your doctor will emphasize the need to take the tablets and behave normally.

Grand mal the sufferer loses consciousness and becomes rigid, followed by twitching or shaking of the body. A child will often urinate and may go red in the face. It may be several minutes before consciousness is regained, followed by several hours of drowsiness.

Petit mal generally affects children between four and sixteen. For a few seconds only there is a loss of consciousness, but the child remains in position, perhaps with the eyes flickering. When the child 'comes to' he or she does not realize anything has happened.

In the UK, a person who has experienced no daytime fits for two years is allowed to drive even when still taking medication.

Spina bifida

This disorder of the nervous system appears to run in families: a woman who has given birth to a spina bifida child has a one in twenty chance of bearing another. A blood test carried out in the fifteenth week of pregnancy can detect the abnormally high levels of alpha-feto-protein (AFP) present when a baby has spina bifida. As the presence of AFP can indicate other conditions as well (such as a multiple birth), a further test may be done. Amniocentesis (drawing off some of the amniotic fluid surrounding the fetus in the uterus) with the help of an ultrasound scan, can confirm the diagnosis. If the result is positive, a termination of pregnancy will be offered.

Spina bifida means 'split spine'. The bones and tissues around the spinal cord fail to develop, leaving nerve fibers and membranes exposed. Spina bifida occulta is a mild defect of little significance, but the most severe forms may result in physical or mental handicap or both, in spite of prompt and sophisticated treatment. For example, an operation after birth may well be necessary to provide protection for the spinal cord. Hydrocephalus (water on the brain) may be present; an operation to drain the fluid into the bloodstream is necessary to avoid brain damage leading to mental retardation. Meningitis is a possible complication.

It depends on the severity of the condition, but children handicapped by spina bifida usually need to attend special schools.

Rhesus disease

This disease is not passed down from generation to generation. It occurs when a woman whose blood group is rhesus negative, and whose partner is rhesus positive, gives birth to a rhesus positive baby. During labor some of the baby's red blood cells pass into the mother's bloodstream. Because their blood groups do not match, she forms antibodies in her bloodstream which persist and affect her second and subsequent babies. These babies will have jaundice, anemia and brain damage, and some do not survive.

Rhesus disease can easily be prevented by halting the formation of antibodies in the mother with an injection of rhesus antibodies from the blood of another person. These 'foreign' antibodies disappear within weeks, so that future babies are unharmed.

Coeliac disease

One in two thousand suffer from this digestive disorder which commonly affects babies, though sometimes it is not evident until adult life. It is due to an intolerance to gluten, a protein found predominantly in wheat and other cereals. The affected person is unable to absorb essential food from the intestines. While a baby's only source of food is milk, the disorder is not evident, but as soon as flour and cereals are introduced into the diet the symptoms appear. The baby does not thrive, is weak and fretful. The abdomen is swollen and the stools are very soft, pale and unpleasantly smelly. If the condition is left untreated vitamin and mineral deficiencies cause anemia, thinning of the bones and other problems. Tests are required to confirm the diagnosis. Eliminating gluten from the diet is essential, but a number of gluten-free products are available and constructing a suitable diet is not difficult: your doctor or health visitor can give detailed advice.

Down's syndrome

Down's syndrome is an abnormality of the brain resulting from a chromosomal abnormality. The normal person has forty-six chromosomes: a person with Down's syndrome has forty-seven. Chromosomes are present in every cell of the body, so physical characteristics are also involved. Muscular tone is poor; the eyes are small and slanting, the nose is small and snub-shaped. In the majority of cases the disorder is of the 'regular' type, where the baby's parents have completely normal chromosomes. Rarely, one or both of the parents has abnormal chromosomes, though they themselves are normal physically and mentally. A blood test on the baby will determine whether or not he or she has inherited

Down's syndrome, so that the parents can be advised of the risks of having more children. The risk of having a 'regular' Down's syndrome child rises with the age of the mother.

As well as mental handicap to varying degrees, Down's syndrome babies are likely to have an abnormal heart. They have a greater tendency to colds and chest infections because of the shape of the nose, which makes them snuffly. Modern antibiotics and surgery have meant that Down's syndrome people have a much greater life expectancy than formerly.

Help from the community is important for families with Down's syndrome children. They are exceptionally good-natured and lively, and many parents attest that their Down's syndrome child has brought them great happiness.

Thyroid deficiency

The thyroid gland is situated at the front of the neck. The hormones it produces are essential for proper growth. When babies are tested for phenylketonuria (page 75) it is routine to test for levels of the thyroid hormone at the same time.

Some babies are born without a thyroid gland. If untreated, mental handicap follows (the condition known as cretinism). Without a positive blood test, the condition is not obvious at first; but soon the baby becomes lethargic, constipated and the cry becomes hoarse as a result of thickened vocal cords. Health clinic staff are trained to note these symptoms. Early treatment is essential to allow the brain to develop correctly and to prevent stunting of physical growth. Some children have a thyroid gland which does not produce enough hormone. They will seem to be developing normally at first, but in the second to third year will show signs of slowing down, dullness and constipation. Their mental capacities are unlikely to have been affected, but again, early diagnosis and treatment is essential.

Cerebral palsy

Cerebral palsy results from brain damage. This can happen at different times and in different ways. For example, in early pregnancy, maternal German measles or other infections can affect brain development: in late pregnancy poor nutrition or, more often, malfunction of the placenta, means that the brain fails to develop completely; the most frequent cause is damage at birth if the oxygen supply to the brain is temporarily cut off. Frequently, no definite cause can be found.

The parts of the brain involved in cerebral palsy are those affecting movement and posture, and depending on which mechanism is affected, the result is either paralysis or stiffness (spasticity) or floppiness in the muscles. Intelligence may or may not be affected (in athetoid cerebral palsy, caused by severe jaundice, it never is). Though the facial expression is likely to be slightly distorted this is not an indication of mental handicap; hearing may be poor; eating and speaking will be difficult because of limited muscle control. In very severe cases, the child may be completely helpless.

There are no drugs to improve muscular control diminished by cerebral palsy. Treatment necessarily involves the work of a range of therapists, including psychologists and social workers, to help and support parents in making their child's life as full as possible, meeting their special needs while encouraging as much independence as is realistic.

Birthmarks

Some birthmarks are caused by abnormalities in the blood vessels. If capillaries (the smallest blood vessels of all) are wider than normal, the skin will look red. Salmon patches or stork bites (see page 10) derive their name from the old fable that babies were delivered down the chimney by a friendly stork whose beak has clasped the human bundle by the nape of the neck. These marks are seen in about a quarter of the population. They are very common on the back of the neck and, less often, on the forehead or upper eyelid. Fortunately, those on the face usually disappear within a few months but on the back of the neck they may remain throughout life.

A port wine stain is less common. It is a permanent, dark red patch visible at birth which is usually flat but may have an uneven surface. These patches sometimes appear on the face, but they do not spread. They only grow as the body grows. As the child gets older, the color may become more purple. Laser therapy may be used to treat the problem, and the recent advances in the tunable dye laster is less likely to cause scarring and is very effective on the pinker stains of children. These lasers are very expensive and treatment is not generally available. However, within a few years, it is likely that the major centers will have these lasers.

Stawberry marks are not usually present at birth, but may appear at any time in the first few weeks of life. A strawberry mark then begins to grow very rapidly and may reach the size of a strawberry, even an apple. The period of growth is not followed by an equally rapid shrinking, taking between four to eight years to disappear altogether. This shrinkage begins when pale patches appear on the mark. These increase in size until only a red rim remains around the now flattened area of skin. This itself disappears eventually. If the mark is on, or close to, the eye it can obscure vision or push onto the eyeball. In this case, surgery may be recommended, but under normal circumstances these marks are left to resolve without any intervention.

Autism

Autism is a rare mental disorder which is difficult to diagnose or to ascribe to a single cause. Some children are born with it, although it may not at first be obvious. The chief characteristic is an inability and unwillingness to communicate with others. These children withdraw into worlds of their own, never playing with others but indulging in repetitive, solitary games, and they insist on monotonous regularity in daily life.

Such behavioral difficulties do not mean that the

autistic child is mentally handicapped; he or she may indeed be brilliantly talented in one area, such as music or mathematics.

The treatment of autism is problematic, since the cause is unknown. The most important factor is therapy by teachers specializing in the field, who have evolved various techniques for 'getting in touch' with individual children and helping them open up to the world.

Jaundice

Many newborn babies have jaundice in the first week of life. This 'physiological jaundice' is easily treated, if necessary, by phototherapy.

Jaundice which does not respond to this treatment and where other symptoms are present may be caused by rhesus disease (see page 77), sickle cell anemia or thalassemia (see page 74) or an infection causing an impairment of liver function. Such infections are usually treatable with antibiotics.

Meningitis and encephalitis

Meningitis and encephalitis: when to worry
If any of the following symptoms, alone or in combination occur, consult your doctor:
• Fever, which may be mild, causing drowsiness or distractedness
• Acute irritability
• Lack of response to stimulus in a small baby
• Tense anterior fontanelle
• Acute headache in an older child
• A neck so stiff that the child cannot touch chin onto chest
• Intolerance of light
• A convulsion

The meninges is the membrane encasing the brain and spinal cord. Meningitis describes inflammation of this membrane. Encephalitis is inflammation of the brain itself. Some cases of meningitis are accompanied by a red skin rash which does not fade if you press it. Meningitis often occurs in outbreaks and from time to time epidemics can affect the community. Antibiotics may be prescribed under these circumstances for children who have been in close contact with a case of meningitis. Only very occasionally is vaccination necessary.

If your doctor suspects meningitis or encephalitis your child will be admitted to hospital immediately. A lumbar puncture to draw off a sample of cerebrospinal fluid will be taken to confirm the diagnosis. Treatment is by prompt administration of antibiotics, complete rest and medication to reduce the fever. Recovery is almost always within days, but a period of convalescence follows.

Although meningitis is very frightening, most cases

will get better without the need for antibiotics. In its mild form, meningitis is one of the complications of mumps.

Dyslexia

Sometimes referred to as 'word blindness', dyslexia is a condition in which a normal child finds it very difficult to read because he or she cannot distinguish the printed symbols, especially those that look alike, such as 'b' and 'd' or 'y' and 'g'. The child's sight is normal and the ability to express himself or herself in speech perfectly adequate. This apparent normality can lead to accusations of laziness and exhortations to try harder. What is really needed is the attention of a teacher specially trained in dealing with reading difficulties. Individual attention, patience and sympathy are crucial in overcoming the problem, but a dyslexic child does not usually need to go to a special school as long as he or she has individual classes and an understanding teacher for the rest of his or her educational needs.

Alternative approaches

The continuum concept

While we may think that crying and babies go together like bread and butter, in other societies it is virtually unknown for a healthy baby to cry. Tears would be understood as a sign of genuine distress or illness, and never as a sign of bad temper. The concept of a 'spoiled' baby, and the idea that 'crying is good for him', would seem mysterious and quite probably barbaric. The parents' only thought would be to remove the cause of unhappiness or pain.

Carrying babies is routine throughout the undeveloped world, and in recent years we have adopted baby carriers for newborn babies. The babies clearly find it reassuring to be carried next to their mother, while the mothers benefit from having a quiet, contented baby.

But this stage, of frequent carrying and close physical contact, soon passes for most babies. It may become inconvenient for the mother, who cannot manage the shopping as well as the baby, or she may find the baby becomes too heavy after the first few weeks.

In other cultures, however, babies are seldom if ever put down or left alone. They are always in the company of an adult, and are carried on their mother's hip or back as she goes about her daily activities. At night, they sleep with her. Breastfeeding is simple. When the baby begins to murmur, the mother need only swing it round to her front for a feed.

Observers have noted that babies raised in this way are relaxed and confident, and sit quietly on a parent's lap without the continual tensing and wriggling we are used to. Their need for movement and activity is in large part satisfied by sharing in the movement of the mother, and she is able to resume her normal activities - housework, gardening, wood and water carrying - with little or no interference from the baby.

Recent medical studies have begun to recognize that this instinctive approach to handling small babies may be far healthier for them, physically as well as emotionally. When a baby cries it is in genuine distress, and hours of panic may suppress the immune system -

contributing, some believe, to Sudden Infant Death Syndrome (SIDS).

Many parents are finding that by taking their child - or children - to bed with them the whole family is able to get a good night's sleep. Hesitation about having a baby or older child in a 'family bed' is a modern worry. Throughout history, and in many other cultures (including Japan) today, sleeping with children is taken for granted. As long as the parents have not been drinking or taking sleeping tablets, this is perfectly safe, even with a newborn baby.

Some researchers into SIDS think that an infant's breathing may be para-sympathetic - in rhythm with the breathing of an adult - and that family sleeping is reassuring to parents and child. Moving a child into his or her own bed can easily wait till he or she is old enough to want to be alone at night.

Extended breastfeeding

Rather than trying to force a child into early independence, giving him or her continual personal contact and care when small and necessarily dependent will result in a preschooler who is confident and emotionally secure.

While new mothers are encouraged to breastfeed their babies, by the time the baby is three or four months old the mothers are being given advice about weaning. Well-meaning friends or relations may ask whether the baby has 'progressed' to a bottle, with an assumption that breast to bottle is a natural progression.

In fact, human beings are designed for long-term lactation: probably four to five years. To feed a child for that length of time is certainly unusual in this country, but it is normal in other parts of the world. Extended breastfeeding has benefits for mother and child.

It is, however, difficult to carry on feeding your baby without sufficient encouragement and support. There are several organizations which give support to breastfeeding mothers, and if you and your child want to continue breastfeeding it is a good idea to get in touch with them. You will then be able to meet other mothers who are doing the same thing.

Every baby is different, and while one child may want to continue nursing until ready for school, another may stop far earlier. Six months seems to be a minimum period for long-term good health. Allowing the child to decide on an appropriate time to stop is called baby-led weaning.

Extending breastfeeding does not interfere with a child's eating solid foods. It provides fluid and nourishment which complement the other foods he or she is eating, and can be supplemented with bottles of water and juice. The child continues to benefit from immunological protection from the mother's milk.

Babies and older children find nursing especially comforting in times of stress or tiredness, and may continue to have a feed at bedtime long after they have given up daytime feeds.

Touch

In the womb, babies have the sides of the womb to push against and a sympathetic medium, the amniotic fluid, to move in. As mothers know, they are extremely active, and can perform all sorts of movements. This activity develops the fetus's muscles and coordination.

Once they are born, however, they struggle helplessly in an unresponsive environment of blankets and empty air. The same purposeful movements are to no avail. This limits their experience and capability, and leads to frustration and fretfulness.

But there are now bodyworkers who are exploring ways of handling infants which will enable them to do more for themselves. Babies can roll and twist, curl, stretch and pull. Unlike dolls, they can respond to and cooperate with your movements. Instead of pushing and pulling, and yanking the baby into position, we can provide a springboard for his or her own movement.

This approach reviews many aspects of the way we handle our children. Frederick LeBoyer pioneered 'birth without violence' and we are now looking at ideas for handling our children with gentleness and respect.

These principles are not limited to use with babies. A guiding nudge which will enable a six-week-old infant to roll over can be used by nurses to move twelve-stone patients. The principle is to give the baby something to push on, in the way he or she used the walls of the womb, instead of being overwhelmed by your superior strength.

Another way of soothing a baby, and developing a closer physical relationship, is by using massage. Although you can attend classes or workshops in baby massage, you don't have to have special training. A warm room, some pure vegetable oil (perhaps scented with a few drops of a natural essential oil like rose or chamomile) and a large towel are all you need. Gentle stroking, generally in towards the heart, forms the basis of massage techniques. This is a wonderful way to soothe a fretful baby, and can become a daily ritual, either after or in place of a bath before bedtime.

Fathers often feel uncertain about how to handle babies, and massage is an ideal way to gain confidence and learn to play with a tiny baby. As the child grows older, the massage session can develop into a romp, and later into soft gymnastics.

Physical confidence

A mother duck doesn't worry about whether her ducklings will follow her as she paddles off across a pond. She knows that they will. This is instinctive behavior for ducklings.

Children, too, are born with an instinct for self-preservation. Surprisingly, they often manage to lose it at an early age. Mothers find themselves chasing a child around the park, admonishing him or her not to go out of sight. A duckling does everything in its power to keep its mother in sight, while many small children seem to have an unerring desire to get lost.

This is not true of children who grow up in a physical setting where there are natural dangers to be avoided. They follow their parents just as a small animal would. Our problem may well arise from the well-meant over-protectiveness which has become the norm in our society.

Children need a considerable degree of personal

freedom in order to develop fully, and the restrictions of modern life have led to a situation in which children are becoming increasingly unfit. They do less well at sports and physical proficiency tests than the children of even a few decades ago. This is thought to be the result of more time spent indoors watching television, and the increased physical limitations caused by heavy traffic and by worries about personal safety.

Providing facilities and opportunities for running, climbing, jumping and cycling is essential. Play places should be as unstructured as possible, to allow children to use their bodies, and test their skills, as well as to encourage the function of imagination.

Besides this, try to avoid inhibiting your child with constant warnings. Children tend, subconsciously, to do whatever is expected of them. Psychologists say that a child hears a warning - 'Be careful, you'll fall down' - as a suggestion or prediction, and subconsciously tries to fulfill the parent's expectations by proceeding to fall.

Children should wear clothing which allows full freedom of movement, and comfortable shoes with good traction for running and climbing. Girls need to develop physical prowess just as much as boys do, if they are to stay healthy and fit throughout their lives. Parental example is important, in this area as in many others. Mothers and fathers who enjoy sport and physical activities will find it easy to get their children off the sofa and onto the playing field. Take up outdoor activities which the whole family can share: cycling, rambling, orienteering or windsurfing.

The more opportunity a child gets to use and test the limits of his or her body, the better he or she will be at it. A child accustomed to climbing will rarely (if ever) fall, because he or she has developed balance and coordination. In any case, a scraped knee is a small price to pay for life-long fitness.

Other children

The ability to develop close relationships in later life is almost inextricably linked to childhood friendships. Some studies suggest that other children are even more important than the mother in a child's emotional development.

The ages of four to ten seem to be crucial in developing emotional health. Isolation during this period (with the television instead of other children) can lead to emotional difficulties in forming adult relationships, and even to psychiatric disorders in later life.

When people lived in extended families or in close communities, children grew up not only with their brothers and sisters but with cousins, grandparents and aunts and uncles. The 'nuclear' family - consisting of a father, a mother and their children - is a recent development. Today's smaller families, of only one or two children, further restrict the companions a child has early in life. When the father is away at work, a child may spend almost all the waking hours alone with mother.

This is not a healthy situation for mother or child. Settling in a community where there are other parents with small children, and finding local coffee circles, playgroups and One O'Clock Clubs are ways of lessening isolation and giving your children those first vital contacts.

The fact that children are not able to play together in a cooperative way until they are three or so does not mean that they do not need other children from the time they are born. Babies are fascinated by other babies. Two-year-olds will often play side by side. As they become older, they begin to play together.

Children need to spend informal time together, not only time at school or organized visits. This can be difficult, depending on where you live and whether there are other children of roughly the same age nearby. Solving this is a complicated issue and needs consideration from local councils and planning authorities as well as parents.

Connected play space where children can mix freely, under parental observation and safe from cars, is needed. An overdependence on toys and television has a great deal to do with not having enough companionship, and you may want to give extra thought to this aspect of provision for your child, whatever age.

Osteopathy

Osteopathy is probably the most widely known and used of alternative therapies, and it can be extremely helpful in improving children's health and development.

This therapy is a system of manipulating bones, muscles and connective tissues to allow proper mechanical alignment of structure, free movement of blood and lymphatic fluids, and the normal transmission of nervous impulses in the body's regulatory systems.

Cranio-sacral therapy is an extremely gentle refinement of standard osteopathic manipulation. It works by releasing subtle restrictions in the connective tissues of the body which hinder the body's natural healing abilities. Cranio-sacral osteopathy is in some ways similar to acupuncture, because it releases restrictions in the flow of energy in the body. Some acupuncturists also use cranial techniques.

The majority of patients who go to osteopaths go because of a bad back, and some women can find them of great value throughout pregnancy. After a difficult labor, an osteopath can help your body to resume its former state of good health, as well as helping a baby who has suffered head moulding or the use of forceps.

Alternative therapists find that they can be helpful with a wide variety of illnesses or difficulties for which conventional medicine offers little relief. Osteopathy is generally a good choice for sleep, learning and emotional problems.

It is important to find an osteopath who specializes in cranio-sacral techniques (if you want this form of treatment, because many osteopaths never use it. You will also want a therapist who has experience in working with children. There are registers of qualified osteopaths, and you can be referred to a practitioner in your area.

Acupuncture

Acupuncture is a Chinese system of medicine which is a safe and effective way of treating a variety of childhood ailments. It has been recognized as a valuable treatment in China since the Song Dynasty (960-1279 AD), and is widely used there today for adults and children. It is becoming more widely known and accepted in the UK, as parents search for alternatives to drugs, and for problems which conventional medicine is unable to help.

Acupuncture is the practice of inserting a fine needle into points on the skin which are along pathways of energy, or chi. Ill health occurs when this energy becomes unbalanced. By directing the energy using the needles it can be strengthened, calmed and balanced.

The needles are inserted for approximately ten seconds, with two to six insertions per treatment. Pressure with a metal probe (called a 'friendly needle') and the use of a warming herb called 'Moxa' are other methods of stimulating the acupuncture points.

Treatments are weekly or fortnightly, and the number required depends both on the condition and the child's response. Most children find acupuncture painless, and enjoy the attention they get during treatment.

Acupuncture does not merely treat the immediate symptoms of an illness but works to strengthen the general health. As a child becomes healthier, he or she feels happier and is better able to cope with difficulties.

The discipline can treat problems for which conventional Western medicine can only offer drugs to relieve the symptoms. Eczema and asthma are two examples. It is useful for a wide range of problems, from teething pain and bedwetting to sleeping and digestive problems.

There are professional organizations of acu-puncurists, and they can refer you to a practitioner in your area. Some therapists specialize in treating children.

Homeopathy

This widely known form of treatment, used by many people including members of the British Royal Family, uses small amounts of herbs and natural extracts, formulating into tiny pills.

Homeopathy works on the principle that 'like cures like'. This means that if a substance causes symptoms similar to those typical of the ailment being treated, it is used to boost the strength of those symptoms because these are the body's positive reaction to illness. This is different from treatment with drugs, the intention of which is to treat, and remove, the symptoms themselves.

Homeopathy aims to stimulate the natural healing process and to improve the body's fundamental defences against illness.

Many wholefood shops and chemists stock one of several ranges of homeopathic remedies. It is possible to treat your children yourself, by reading the labels carefully and experimenting with the alternatives for a particular ailment. Homeopathy, like other alternative therapies, believes that there are a number of cures for a single ailment, and that the correct one depends on the individual.

There are also a variety of guides to homeopathic remedies, which suggest a basic 'medicine kit' to keep at home.

Self-treatment is completely safe, because the remedies are only minute quantities of the active agent, in sugar pills. Nonetheless, parents need to be cautious about using any treatment too freely. It may become easier to give a child a few of these little pills than to examine the reasons for, say, recurrent tantrums. Pill taking for an instant cure is not part of an alternative approach to health care, which does not believe in the 'magic bullet'.

For a more comprehensive and expert approach, you can visit a homeopath or a homeopathic doctor. Many children respond well to homeopathic treatment throughout childhood, and avoid taking drugs altogether.

Immunization

There still some parents who are concerned about routine immunization and who need better information about the health risks before deciding to have their children vaccinated.

A Health Education Council leaflet on immunization points out that 'any child who does not have the (measles) vaccine is virtually certain to catch (the disease)...So there's a clear choice between having the measles or having the vaccine.'

A doctor in Australia has used vitamin C and zinc supplements to boost immune function before giving vaccines to vulnerable children, and the previously high infant mortality in the group virtually disappeared. If you decide to go ahead with vaccination, you might want to give your baby extra vitamin C and some multimineral drops containing zinc.

Fluoride

Until the 1930s, fluoride was considered a poison. At that time, the world's expanding steel and aluminium industries had serious problems in disposing of the soluble fluoride waste which was being generated by their industries.

By coincidence, a chemist employed by the sugar industry (which wanted to find a way of reducing tooth decay without lowering sugar consumption) noticed that the ingestion of small amounts of fluoride (naturally occurring in the well water in certain areas) seemed to limit decay.

After a time and with the appropriate legislation, instead of being fined for contaminating water supplies with fluoride, the aluminium and steel industries were able to sell the waste fluoride to water authorities.

You can keep your child's teeth in good condition without fluoride by sticking to a diet low in sugar and high in minerals, along with proper brushing habits. And if, after further reading, you still want your children to have fluoride, why not use fluoride drops in a prescribed dose rather than rely on random intake from toothpaste or tap water?

Safe food

Chemical additives, which include colorings, flavorings and preservatives, are by no means the only dangerous chemicals in our food. The case of Alar, a growth promoter used on apples, highlighted the way even 'healthy' foods like fresh fruit and vegetables contain

Until our food is safe, here are some tips to help you safeguard your children:

• Thoroughly wash produce. Plain water or a mild solution of biodegradable washing-up liquid and water will remove some, but not all, of the surface pesticide residues.
• Peel produce. This means losing valuable nutrients, but will completely remove surface residues.
• Buy domestically-grown produce and seasonal fruits and vegetables, which probably contain fewer pesticide residues.
• Press for comprehensive labelling of fresh fruits and vegetables.
• Buy organic produce and other foods. Best of all, grow your own.

traces of the highly dangerous chemicals used in modern agriculture.

Government 'safety' levels have been found to be seriously flawed. The Ministry of Agriculture has admitted that pesticides in common use were inadequately tested and that new studies are needed. Many health workers, as well as environmental groups, point out that there is no such thing as a safe level of these chemicals - pesticides, herbicides and fungicides are, by their nature, poisons. Fortunately, organic agriculture offers us a practical alternative.

Food sensitivities

The most common food sensitivities are to wheat and to cow's milk. Some babies are so sensitive that they react to these foods even while breastfed, if the mother consumes them in large quantities. The usual symptoms include digestive upset or colic, and breathing difficulties because the body reacts to foreign substances by building up mucus to protect itself.

Some parents avoid giving wheat or cow's milk to babies under the age of one, by using rye, barley and rice breads and cereals, and by continuing breastfeeding for as long as possible. Goat and sheep milk do not present the same problems, and can be used in place of cow's milk throughout childhood if necessary.

Naturopaths and clinical ecologists specialize in treating these problems, and will advise on using a rotation diet to discover which food groups a child is sensitive to. It is sometimes possible to desensitize the child over a period of time.

Nappies

The thirty per cent of parents who still use cloth nappies (the other seventy per cent have gone over to plastic-and-paper 'disposables') are in the vanguard, in these days of Green living. 'Disposable' nappies are a prime example of the waste which has become an accepted part of the way we live - and which we now know has to change.

The trouble with 'disposables' is that they are not disposable. One estimate suggests that some five per cent of all domestic waste is composed of soiled nappies. Modern sanitation and plumbing was designed to separate fecal matter from other waste, which goes into landfill sites or is burned, but with the advent of 'disposables' this system has broken down, and huge amounts of fecal matter is now treated as household rubbish, instead of being processed through the sewage system.

'Disposable' nappies contribute to the depletion of limited timber and petroleum reserves, and while the paper is no longer chlorine-bleached in most brands, some children are sensitive to the chemicals, perfumes and even to the plastics which are used on 'disposable' nappies. And the use of plastic coverings, whether on a 'disposable' or with terries, is a prime contributor to the modern problem of nappy rash.

Using terries or other cloth nappies is far less expensive than buying 'disposables'. A baby gets through at least five thousand nappies, at a cost of a thousand pounds. Even taking washing and machine drying into account, cloth nappies run to less than half that - and subsequent babies can use the same supplies.

Nylon pants wash easily, and there are several types of attractive woollen covers on the market, too. These covers fit over cotton nappies. Some of the covers are pinless, with velcro fastenings, and rival 'disposables' in terms of changing ease.

With an automatic washing machine, using cloth nappies should take you no more than an extra ten minutes a day, and you no longer have to haul huge bags of 'disposables' home, or find your dustbin full of unpleasant, unsightly rubbish.

Making the choice to use a product which is slightly more time-consuming is one which more and more parents are willing to make because of their concern about the world they will leave to their children.

Other titles in the series

Your Active Body (ISBN 0 245-55070-4)
Your Sex Life (ISBN 0 245-55067-4)
Your Heart and Lungs (ISBN 0 245-55069-0)
Your Pregnancy and Childbirth (ISBN 0 245-55068-2)
Your Mind (ISBN 0 245-60008-6)
Your Diet (ISBN 0 245-60009-4)
Your Skin (ISBN 0 245-60010-8)
Your Child (ISBN 0 245-60011-6)

Available, Autumn 1990
Your Female Body (ISBN 0 245-60012-4)
Your Senses (ISBN 0 245-60013-2)
A-Z of Conditions and Drugs (ISBN 0 245-60014-0)

Useful organizations

*Family Planning Information
Service
27-35 Mortimer Street
London W1N 7RJ*

*National Childbirth Trust
9 Queensborough Terrace
London W2 3TB*

*Natural Family Planning
Centre
Queen Elizabeth Medical
Centre
Edgbaston
Birmingham B15 2TG*

*Pregnancy Advisory Service
11-13 Charlotte Street
London W1P 1ND*

*Gingerbread
2nd Floor
35 Wellington Street
London WC2E 7BN*

*Women's Health Information
Centre
52-54 Featherstone Street
London EC1Y 8RT*

*Stillbirth and Neonatal Deaths
Society
28 Portland Place
London W1N 3DE*

*Society of Homoeopaths
47 Canada Grove
Bognor Regis
West Sussex PO21 1OW*

*Council for Acupuncture
(umbrella group for the main
colleges)
Suite One
191A Cavendish Squre
London W1M 9AD*

*General Council and Register
of Osteopaths
21 Suffolk Street
London SW1Y 4HG*

*National Institute of Medical
Herbalists
41 Hatherley Road
Winchester
Hampshire SO22 6RR*

*MGI PRIME HEALTH
Private Medical Insurance
Prime House
Barnett Wood Lane
Leatherhead
Surrey KT22 7BS
0372 386060*